Hope's Work

Hope's Work

Facing the future in an age of crises

DAVID GEE

DARTON·LONGMAN+TODD

First published in Great Britain in 2021 by
Darton, Longman and Todd Ltd
1 Spencer Court
140–142 Wandsworth High Street
London SW18 4JJ

© 2021 David Gee

ISBN: 978-1-913657-03-1

The right of David Gee to be identified as the Author of this work has been asserted in
accordance with the Copyright, Designs and Patents Act 1988.

A catalogue record for this book is available from the British Library.

Designed and produced by Judy Linard
Printed and bound in Great Britain by Bell & Bain, Glasgow

Virgin water tumbling tumbling down the hill

First the storm and then the time when all is still

All will follow follow follow

All in balance when the earth does as she will

Peggy Seeger, from The Mother

CONTENTS

PREFACE

This book goes digging for hope, in search of its roots, its soil, and the subterranean stream that gives it life. I decided to write it after hearing many people, who have for a long time involved themselves in the life of the world around them, confess a fading faith for its future. They have wondered in whispers whether their work has any point at all. I know the same doubts, having worked in the peace movement for two decades only to witness the nations of the world deepen their investment in war and accelerate their race to dominate people and planet.

How to respond? My first instinct was to insist on the promise of the life we all share, as it comes to us unbidden every day, like a gift. I would have loved to write that book, but a billion people worldwide live in slums, forced to the edge of existence by a system of economic violence. Hope has to be worthy of their world, too, and speak to this age of crises. We set out, then, not with life as beauty, though it is and can be beautiful, but with its violation – by Western societies in particular and their more comfortable class especially, in which I myself am steeped.

Violence is, I think, hope's problem. This book tries to accept the fact of it, but also to move through it to a hope that can survive it – and face it. In the end, I believe we are left with a shaken-down, conscious hope, which is, it turns out, the promise of the life we all share. I hope that you will feel the same.

The book opens and ends with a story. In between, eight chapters explore various energies that feed the work of hope. And at the back, a section of notes reviews the sources used. We begin with a myth of beginnings.

PROLOGUE. IN THE BEGINNING

Listen on! Listen on! This is the truth of it! Here's hope's tale, now as it was in the beginning.

When there was no heaven, no earth, no height, no depth, no name, Tiamat the dragon was on the move. She roiled with Apsu and her spawn shivered out, green and true, to swim the cavernous blue. Dawn broke bright. Quickly her offspring multiplied, reached the shore, scurried under stones. With a shriek a million wings were slung skyward.

As the creatures swarmed Apsu took affront: 'Their manners revolt me, day and night,' he moaned. 'My will is to destroy them, all of their kind, and we shall have peace.'

Tiamat's heart worked hard. 'Why must we destroy the children that we made? If their ways are troublesome, let us wait a little while.'

Hope's Work

Well, the gods were all at sea. They wanted the dragon dead but none could even hold her eye. Then one named Marduk, proud and absolute in action, struck a strange and terrible bargain with them: ' Make me first of all of you, now and forever let my word be law and I shall slay the one that vexes us. Then I, not you, will decide the world's nature, the things to come.'

The gods wrung their hands but said all right. Marduk took his net and trawled the deep, scooped up the dragon and hauled her in. This is what the old clay has to say: ' He wrapped her up, stopped her mouth, and shot his arrow that split the belly, pierced the gut and cut the womb.' Tiamat's waters spilled and sank under the sand.

There Marduk thrust his blade. Black naphtha oozed from the wound. ' Build my city,' he thundered, ' it shall be Babylon, the home of the gods.' There he'd have his tower built, heaven's gate, but first he laid his hands on a craven god, chopped him up, and put the chunks together anew: ' Blood to blood I join, blood to bone I form, and its name is Man.' And Man he divided between men of worth and poor men and slaves, without a word about the women.

Marduk took the throne of lapis lazuli. The grand scribe kissed the royal ring. On one side stood the high priest with the marshal of the army, on the other the taxman with the hooded executioner. At the sound of the horn and drum, pigeons and pigs were brought for burning, the whole crowd bowed to the ground. Well, almost. A few of us said no, we had our own song to sing, and we lived from then in the city's shadows.

Walls were raised, taxes too. The slaves and the soil were worked hard. These were times of plenty. Soon, so the scribe said, the king would weigh the world in just one hand, and with a word whirl the stars about his crown.

The slaves were first to see the signs. The soil was left no rest. The rains mauled it to mush, it caked and cracked in the white heat of the day. Southerly storms lifted it as dust and dumped it in the desert.

Out went the army and out again, and harder won were

its victories. The ranks returned at night, famished and ill at heart.

By now the king's face sagged, his mouth drooled. Papery drapes of skin hung lank from the same arms, so the tablets tell, that stretched Tiamat's carcass across the face of the earth.

Well, the writing was on the wall. One morning we just walked out, a motley lot of every hue with nothing left to burn but our hearts. We pitched our tents among the old olives, by a tumbling spring. We worked together, broke bread together there.

In and out of the city we went, in with the birds at dawn, and out with the birds at dusk, and in between we scratched about with them in the city square. The priests called us heathens, for we lived in the open. The scribes called us barbarians, for our speech sounded strange.

One time one of us fetched a fistful of sand and turned to the crowd: 'This earth grows tired of the plough. It aches with the weight of war. Hope dries up. But listen on!

In the beginning

The dew of the heavens waits for you even now. Hold faith!'

The speech struck a chord. In some the spirit quickened and a few had great openings. Others hardened their hearts, angry and afraid. They cheered when the king's counsel, a man of gold and guile, held forth against us: 'For the great god Marduk, great lord, heroic, eminent, exalted, lord of everything, lord of lords, august judge who makes decisions for the world of people, lord of the lands, lord of Babylon who rules only to bless, conquers only to spare ....'

On and on he went like that, and finally, 'Babylon, pearl of the earth! Why do you stumble? Beware the heathen for Tiamat lies upon that barbarian tongue! Have you forgotten your foe is afoot, eager to enter your houses and your women? Has he not slain your brothers? Do not kiss his cheek! Do not be found fools for peace! The world slips and slithers to the chaos that was before Marduk. The strong shall be saved and the rest must drown. Build up your walls, whet your spears, and seek again your majesty, as it was in the beginning.'

Hope's Work

In the end, the enemies of Marduk cracked his castle open. A new king took the lofty place of power: 'It was I, and not Marduk, who slew the dragon for the people's sake.' The imperial scribe was first to kiss the victor's ring: 'Noble avenger,' he pleaded, 'allow your servant to record your victory on the royal stele.'

And what of the multitudes? Year after year, as fish flit here and there, going nowhere, so the people drifted downriver towards the bitter sea.

As for us, the remnant, we wandered west in search of a new land. One day the sun rose and there it was, a marvel. None had seen the like – a silvery wall, high poles topped by an empty eye, chariots on the wind spitting fire, long lines of ragged folk waiting at the gates, and such towers within that they scraped the sky itself. By now our bones were hollow, our strength as sleek as a wing. Lifting, lifting, we followed the starlings in.

In the beginning

A thousand tales tell the beginning of the world. The one we are supposed to remember – the authorised version of events – was pressed into clay thousands of years ago: the god-king kills the she-dragon to make way for the grand hopes of civilisation. The myth has belonged ever since to the kings, generals, high priests, and merchantmen who rule the world. Today we paint it on primary school walls: St George lances a dragon's heart for all our helpless sakes. All that preserves our ordered world from chaos, so the story goes, is the lone, male, pale, aristocrat hero. That his violence wins our peace is the first law of civilisation, of Babylon.

But look again. The story begins with the murder of a mother by an arrow to her womb, simply because she inspires fear in the men-gods of civilisation. At the sound of the drum, we are supposed to bow to the ground in gratitude, but what if the dragon is not the enemy of the peace but the body of wildness itself, the wellspring of the world, the natural magic of all its terrors and wonders, which once had been our home? And what if George is not the underdog hero of civilised order but just another over-armed assassin, a man with a talent for killing? Or, more likely, what if high-born George just follows news of the battle from a concrete bunker, while a band of working-class infantrymen from Barnsley do his dirty work on the other side of the world? And what if the well-kept village that George protects is the colony of an imperial power? What if that village, town, city, society, civilisation, is draining the forest of its life and corralling its people to participate? Then George the dragon-slayer is not a saint after all, but a murderer.

The word 'dragon' comes from an ancient root, *derk*, for 'sight' or perhaps 'piercing gaze', suggesting a wild thing that cannot be looked in the eye. Once our ancestors had cleared space in the wild to settle their village, they learnt to dread the surrounding wildness. It comes back, out of a cave, out of the woods, out of our dreams, as the dragon that we thought was slain. That dragon – dark, green, and usually female – still rises in civilisation's fears of all it cannot tame. Killed and reborn thousands of times, the dragon is forever George's quarry, for like any fear we cannot face it will not die. The terrible cost of keeping it at bay has been the warrior-king's rule. From his fortress city, he fashions humankind as his servants, enslaves the soil and sea, and keeps on grasping.

In the beginning

Ancient Babylon, built to last forever, is gone, all its grand hopes fallen away. The city is 'just dust' today, according to the oil company that runs three pipelines through its half-buried ruin to feed our new Babylon with the same, ancient oil. Its heroic story is now inscribed in newspapers owned by billionaires. Marduk is the strongman autocrat or corporate CEO. St George is the 'special forces' soldier blowing a hole in a faraway family home at night, the border guard strip-searching the undocumented migrant, the drone that circles the sky all day in a foreign land. And if George has not lost his soul completely to the machinery of harm, he will be sick at heart and searching himself. In the small hours he will see again the eyes of the children he held at gunpoint as their fathers were hooded and led away. The old myth will well up from his unconscious, seize him in his dreams, and startle him awake.

Meanwhile, civilisation's violence wins it no rest. It fears the unfamiliar, pointing to those in its midst it once called barbarian, but 'barbarians', from ba-ba for 'babble', are simply the people whose language sounds strange. They tell their own tales of doubt and dissent, not on stone tablets but around a fire, under the open sky or huddled in the shadows of Babylon's tower. In their stories they remember who they really are, their hearts burn, and still they hold their hope amid the world of Marduk. Their stories told, they grow ready to look the world in the eye and, wherever they may find themselves, begin again.

1. LOVE

Hope as commitment.

The glass and steel angles of the brand-new shopping mall shimmer in the morning sun. Starlings flit across the airy portico, over the turned-down heads of the people streaming in and out. In just a blink of history, moss might line these colonnades and trees crash up through the vaulted ceiling. Already pushing at the foundations are the roots of weeds – nature's extraordinary hopefulness – but today the concrete is new, yet to crack. Today the mall towers over the town as a gleaming icon of civilisation at work. Today it radiates a dream of progress, as if newer shops meant a better life, a better town, a better society. And yet most of the shoppers moving through its arcades, so surveys say, are losing their faith in the future.

In societies like ours, preoccupied with power and wealth,

optimism once seemed to border on a religion. The 'white heat' of technology would bring free energy, cheap food, immaculate cities, and robot factories to release us from the bonds of hard work. Roadside adverts touted a fair-weather future of better TVs, bigger cars, longer holidays, even vacuum cleaners that would clean the living room by themselves. Standing though we did one four-minute nuclear warning away from annihilation – in fear of the same technological progress that was supposed to liberate us – our societies would still anticipate better things to come. The future would be bright, the message went, so let others do the worrying; take refuge from today in a fantasy of tomorrow.

Now our societies face a complex of crises which have long been allowed to deepen. Economic injustice, over-consumption, and political exclusion are driving famine and mass migration, swelling slums, and sliding the world into wars that repeat without end. On the horizon loom ecological collapse, economic meltdown, and political chaos. A contagious virus easily overruns civilisation because its body is already weakened by over-urbanised populations, runaway air travel, immunity-sapping lifestyles, and underfunded health systems. That we need to change our ways, especially in a rich country, especially in a town with a shopping mall stuck in its a heart, is obvious. But an affluent overclass, heavily invested in business as usual, straddles a global underclass of most of the world's people. While billionaires prepare to future-proof their interests, the rest of the world flounders.

The urgency of our situation might yet quicken our collective spirit, and there are signs of it, but it appears that our societies have yet to find the courage to move in common. For those willing to 'do the worrying', familiar methods of social change – letters to parliamentarians, union solidarity, direct action – seem frustratingly thin next to the power of showboat politicians, mass media, and big business. Every humane effort can seem to ricochet off an unmoving edifice of elite power and public indifference.

Perhaps this accounts for a common loss of optimism, but the loss of hope is different. Hope lives not by optimism's confidence in tomorrow, but by a feeling for what is worth living for today. If hope is hard to come by, it is not because the far horizon has darkened, but because of a fading sense, here and now, of what our lives and societies are for. And if we are uncertain of what we live for in the present, how can we live for a future worthy of the word? Instead, losing trust in the world, unsure of what we want, and turning away from the future, hope dries up.

Then fear calls the shots. Walls go up in Palestine, Calais, Texas. A strongman in Washington or Moscow promises to restore 'this great nation' to bygone glory by fixating on 'immigrants', 'terrorists', and 'rogue states' as the fantasy causes of its unease. The political establishment does all it can to keep the economic system 'growing' and climb the 'league table of global power'. Media barons look down from above, scoff at climate science, cheer on the latest war, and scowl at 'illegals', 'jobless scroungers', and 'teenage jihadis'. Meanwhile, the shopping mall is still the place to be on a Saturday afternoon, funnelling our money to a corporate king as it spews out carbon, plastic, and muzak. For hundreds of millions of people, even some passing by the shopping mall of a rich country, the horizon that looms largest is the coming evening: Will I eat tonight? Will my children eat?

On a bitter day, the world is just a wall to bang a head against, nothing more; anyone who cares about our common fate must wonder whether hope has any reason. Dead end.

Let's begin again, not with where hope dies in the deluge, but with somewhere hope lives against the odds: a prison.

Years ago, while working with inmates on a nonviolence course, we would ask them: 'What matters most to you?' Sometimes we put it another way: 'What do you really love?' Sometimes: 'What would you die for?' The replies were always of the same kind: my partner, my children, mum, dad. Some named their faith, some their football team, but no one said shopping. The inmates were subsisting in a grey prison carefully designed to strip away the things that make life worth living. But they still knew whom and what they really loved and might be worth dying for. They knew too that whatever is worth dying for must also be worth living for, even in a prison – especially in a prison.

Few in jail enjoy the easy optimism that says life will work itself out, but for those who know what they live for, hope is with them. Prison inmates around the world remind themselves of it by taking lumps of toothpaste to stick up photos of the people they care about most. The same reminders stand in frames on the endless ranks of office desks in city skyscrapers and are stashed in the breast pockets of soldiers on the battlefield.

In a search for hope, remembering the people who mean the most to us is a natural place to start, but even tyrants keep family photos on their desks. For sure, the people close to us will mean more to us than strangers ever will, but they are not worth more. When hope is confined to the people we like it has nothing to set against the violation of the stranger, the earth, and anything else beyond the nearest of horizons. A humane hope has to reach outward, past what is comfortably familiar towards the conviction that every person is a world entire – that the dignity of the unmet stranger carries no less value than that of the closest friend. When people cram into a raft to seek asylum on distant shores, an unthinking clamour shouts, 'Let them drown.' But to an empathic imagination, and by the simple reason of justice, their lives matter; they too are worthy of love.

Here, the word 'love' points through and past affection, as a feeling for what has worth, towards commitment, as acting for what has worth. Love is something you do, and what really makes it love is that you will do it even when feelings of affection are absent. We might imagine that such love is rare, but it is everywhere that violence has no dominion. It is there in farmers who have grown to love the land; in teachers who believe in every student; in musicians whose song runs through them like a river; in nurses, builders, gardeners, and cooks who make their work a kind of giving; and in mothers and fathers who tend daily to the wellbeing of their children. Even our *hello!* from 'hale be thou!', wishes wholeness and health for one another, as do the Hebrew *shalom!* and the Arabic *as salaam alaikum!* These greetings belong to the mostly unconscious love that inaugurates everyday encounters all around the world, not least among friends meeting outside the shopping mall today.

A society that moved by the same principle by striving to honour every person as sharing the worth of all humanity, would be organised radically differently from Babylon's ways of coercion and control. It would not brook billionaires or build up the war machine, nor would it seek justice in the punishment centres we know as prisons or put a shopping mall in the middle of every town, for all these institutions live parasitically by draining the life they touch. But our societies are what they are. An individual or a community trying to live by love, committed to learning the work of hope, believes in society too much to condemn it, and doubts it too much to fall into step with it. Hope's work is a journey of tension, conflict, and cost.

Whenever I reach for an example, I remember wartime conscientious objectors: those who refuse orders to kill even at risk of their own death. In the First World War, when army recruitment posters depicted Britain as heroic St George, Germany was drawn as the dragon, and its people as barbarians carting off British women. The German government pulled the same trick, casting Britain as the dragon to sell the same unthinking certainty that only their victory, not Britain's, could impose order on chaos. The aristocrat generals on both sides of the war hoped their posters would convince farmers and factory workers to kill and die for them in the mud of Flanders. While young men signed up in their thousands and most of the rest were conscripted without much complaint, a few said no.

In Britain, the No-Conscription Fellowship were determined to 'deny the right of any Government to make the slaughter of our fellows a bounden duty'. 'All of us,' they wrote, 'believe in the value and sacredness of human personality.' To the objectors in Britain, Germany, and elsewhere, the unknown stranger waiting for them on the battlefield was not an enemy, but kin. To will him dead would be to treat him as less than a human being worthy of love. It would also be, for the objectors' part, to behave as less than human beings with a duty to love. From their point of view, the killing would be an offence against self and other alike, a double betrayal. Accordingly, their conscientious objection was an act of committed love: a conscientious affirmation of the humanity of all people. That meant refusing to kill, but also readiness for hope's work: 'to sacrifice as much in the cause of the world's peace as our fellows are sacrificing in the cause of the nation's war'. Behind their 'no' was a 'yes': a conviction of the worth of all human beings, and with this they went into conflict, not against the enemy soldier but against war itself.

All this was uncomfortable for a state at war, which met the objectors with fear, loathing, and punishment. On all sides of the war, most objectors were conscripted anyway or starved and tortured as cowards for refusing to join the violence that scythed through Europe's youth. And still their solidarity with the stranger is reborn in every war among those who first widen the horizon of their hopes to include all people as radically equal, and then gather the extraordinary courage to accept the costs that follow.

Even the principle of universal human fellowship will not carry us far enough in the work of hope unless it reaches the earth itself, by the grace of which we live. Just as ancient Babylon so overworked its soils that they became salty and sterile, ecocide shames our own age. After the First World War, the machines moved in to colonise the fields, first in America. There, a tradition of small-scale farming had cultivated the land with care, much as native peoples had done before their dispossession, but the lords of industry brandished title deeds as proof the earth was theirs. Slowly, the north American continent, already stolen by white men from the people who belonged to it for centuries, was being stolen again, this time from nature itself.

Among those who sounded a prophetic warning was the pioneering naturalist, Aldo Leopold. He pointed to two futures of society's relationship with the land. In one, the earth offers no more than raw material and the farm is just a factory making products for sale. In the other, the farm is 'a harmonious balance between plants, animals, and people; between the domestic and the wild; between utility and beauty'. The first is a future in which people live aloof from the earth, take it over, and rule it. In the second, people participate intimately in the earth's ways, care for its fertility as a sacred gift, and strive to meet their needs with the discipline of self-limitation. As Aldo had foreseen, corporate America cleared the wild places for today's endless miles of megafarms and monocrops. Conscientious land-workers have had to watch the outsize machinery of global capital drain the life from the soil, leaving the rains to maul it to mush and the southerlies to lift it as dust and dump it in the desert.

Behind Aldo's two futures, and behind the manifesto of the No Conscription Fellowship, is the query that all prophecy carries: What matters? Put another way: What are we committed to? And again: What do we really love? The query is so basic to human life that it comes bound with another: Who am I really, and what is my life *about*? And what is our society *for*? To dwell on these queries is to face that wholly simple, wholly demanding question: What does this mean for what I do next? For the well-grounded land worker, as for the conscientious objector, the deeply hopeful, deeply unsettling answer is to love what is worthy of love, step out of violent ways, and turn to face them down.

Like all prophecy, Aldo's words doubt their listeners and at the same time believe in them. They confront us in the deeply harmful ways in which we are steeped, and at the same time affirm us as humane human beings who have it in us to choose well, or at least choose better. His prophecy of two futures — one turned towards life, the other towards death — neither condones nor condemns, but asks and invites, leaving the way open for hope.

2. PROMISE

Hope chosen.

I meet Basma for the first time in Liverpool, where she has arrived from Libya as a refugee. When we ask about each other and I mention that I am writing about hope, she says with sudden vigour: 'Hope is something you make every day.'

Basma takes me back to 2011, when NATO bombing has pitched Libya into chaos, which Islamist insurgents are exploiting. Her brother Ahmed, 17, has joined a militia to try to stop them from overrunning his country, and is soon killed. At the time Basma is playing dutiful wife to an ambitious man, she tells me, but Ahmed's death shakes her. She wonders what message the tragedy might have for her. 'What was he trying to tell us?'

'I learnt from my little brother that we are dead if we are unable to make hope,' says Basma, 'or if we become prey to fear'. To hope is to act – this is her brother's message – and so Basma plunges into her people's struggles. Her domineering husband opposes her at every step until eventually she leaves him: 'Enough to a lie!' she tells herself. One day, insurgents come to burn down her house and she flees with her two young daughters under heavy gunfire. For weeks, Basma and her children roam from city to city, spending most of the time in the desert until they cross into Tunisia and from there to Britain to claim asylum. Today she cares alone for her children, studies law during the day with no state support, and works in the few gaps that remain to pay for it all, sometimes as a cleaner, sometimes in a fish-and-chip shop. Her brother's death has left her with his determination to stand by people in need, which means, for her, training to be a human rights lawyer.

When I ask Basma what hope means for her, she says, 'You have to face the tragedy of the world.' This, I think, is hope's test, and the tragedy to be faced is violence: the vindictive parent or sibling, the rapacious corporation, the cavalier grandstanding of the superpower state, the designed-in deprivation of poverty, the trammelling of the earth, and every other way that we cause harm, normalise it, even celebrate it. Driving this violence are the seductive, life-denying forces that bear down on all our choices: patriarchy (if you can dominate then dominate), consumer-capitalism (if you can take then take), racism (if you can spit on others then spit). Add to these the countless daily pressures that can suffocate hope, not least the grinding poverty that millions of people have been abandoned to. Such are the forces that cause humanity to collapse into, as Arundhati Roy expresses it, 'brokenness, numbness, uncertainty, fear, the death of feeling, the death of dreaming … the absolute relentless, endless, habitual, unfairness of the world'. Hope, then, is work: face the torment, mourn the losses, resist the violation of what deserves to be loved. We are bound to flinch before all that hope urges, but also to try, at least, not to turn away.

What can tragedy be faced with? What is strong enough, true enough, alive enough? When Basma and I next meet, she tells me about Mansur, a friend jailed without trial for trying to persuade his fellow

Libyans to stop killing each other. For five long years Mansur was stuck in a cell and tortured routinely. When Basma asked him later what had kept him going for so long, cut off as he was from family and friends, his answer amazed her: 'He told me he saw the sun come up each morning and felt the earth was alive.' Evidently, all the violence pitched against Mansur did not rob him of his feeling for the world as a promising place, nor his determination to make a home for that truth in his daily life, even in his barren cell. The sun rising over the earth was an experience strong enough, true enough, alive enough to carry him through. This was 'the secret of his steadfastness', Basma says. One morning, a NATO plane came in from the horizon to bomb his prison to bits, but Mansur somehow survived the attack and fled the rubble. He is now back with his broken country's struggle to move forward.

If hope's test is to face the world as a tragic place, it cannot give up on it as a place of promise; where life is worth living for even, in Mansur's case, behind the bars of a prison cell. The worth and promise of the world, there in every leaf and every greeting; and for Mansur in the rising sun, and for Basma in her children crossing the Libyan desert with her, breathes life into hope's work. That the world remains promising even after all our violence is hope's justification, however long its odds.

Indeed, it is hope's point. For Basma's part, her hope is stronger than it has ever been because 'through struggle, life becomes imperative, more valuable'. That is not to glorify, ever, the life-denying violence that she has had to face. It is to be thankful for the insistence to live – and to live well – that her struggle has brought her to.

What if we too were to gather our lives and societies around all that makes the world a promising place? I put it to Basma that so many well-off people in the Western world talk about the future in tones of despair or indifference, and she says without a moment's pause: 'You're too comfortable here.' She is thinking of people who, having done well for themselves, withdraw to leafy suburbs, cushioned from the world's tragedies but also cut off from its promise. But she is also pointing at the consumer-capitalist script that makes such a retreat from the world the goal of the good life.

The script is familiar enough: achieve in school, get a paying job, start a family, get promoted, buy a house, a car, holiday abroad, a bigger house, a better car, a longer holiday … and so on. You shall give to those in need but remain afraid of them, says the script, and be generous with your friends but resent taxes. You shall tell brands apart but not trees; the script has nothing to say about trees. You shall improve yourself and ascend the pecking order, but never quite reach the feeling of being good enough. You shall crave affirmation but scoff silently when 'true love' is mentioned. You shall know the planet is dying but push the thought away. You shall progress and be congratulated but nothing in the script will remind you that all that is good is a gift, and if you forget to give thanks the script will not notice. And when dusk falls, that bird singing from the tallest branch might be a blackbird, or a song thrush, or whatever; you might wish you had troubled to wonder which and to know its ways.

Meanwhile, says the script, the nation shall pride itself as generous abroad and democratic at home, but ignore the exploitation of other peoples, the economic suppression of its own, and the litany of invasions and massacres that it has no wish to answer for. A rich country shall take pride in its power while passing over deep inequalities among its people. If ours sells destruction to despots and fences out the foreigners, this is the price of security, the script says: export violence to import peace, for civilisation itself depends on it. And so does your hamburger. If you want McDonald's, so writes a champion of global capital, Thomas Friedman, then you had better get used to having McDonnell Douglas, the multinational maker of war machines, because: 'The hidden hand of the market will never work without a hidden fist.'

The first and last of the script's victims is the earth, which bears our violence without complaint but not without hurt, and we are killing it. The more we exhaust the hospitality of its soils and seas, the harder we squeeze it to give up what is left. We ram from the ground the last of its ancient energy and bodge upgrades for its genetic ingenuity, as if it has not been generous enough. The earth, our living, breathing home, is reduced to 'the environment', addressed by the script in the barren language of 'resources', 'stocks' and 'yields'. A contagious virus is an 'enemy' to be defeated like any other: in a 'war'.

As it is, the promise that the imprisoned Mansur found in the rising sun barely infiltrates Babylon's spacious shopping arcades, where the earth's nearest star is just a stage light for a drama without a story — for the exercise of our liberty in retail outlets. And if our screaming newspaper headlines are a guide, then the violence that needs to be reckoned with appears to most of us as just a threat to keep at bay. Our societies fret, build walls, box ourselves in, send out soldiers to keep some imagined dragon back – the greater our power, the lower we cower, and hope dries up.

Listening to people who, like Basma, 'make hope every day', it strikes me that hope's work has no script for success, and yet she and Mansur have not gone unguided. When I hear their stories, I sense what the artist Agnes Martin once called the 'pull of life', which tugs at the elbow, reminding us of who we can be, that choices are still to be made, that the future is still to be lived into. In Basma's own words, hope has been 'a dim feeling inside me seeking to exist' – in a world, it seems, that is never quite ready for it.

Perhaps this is our collective situation as a society, too, caught between a heart-hardening script of a violent system, and the pull of life, its invitation to be, and the possibility of learning to live as if for the first time. My father's years as a Hull trawlerman serve as a kind of parable. It was the 1950s and industrial fishing was booming, says Sam. You just trawled the deep with a net and scooped the fish up, bulldozing the ecosystem as you went, and then hauled in the riches. One in every five fish were gutted and iced for sale, he says; the rest were thrown overboard, where they would thrash and die on the surface because their swim bladders had burst in the trawl. Sam is a kind man, so naturally he rues what he was part of: 'You don't think about it; you detach yourself from the distress you're causing.' The North Sea stocks were soon gone, so Hull's trawler fleet pushed into the Arctic Circle until those shoals were barely worth the chase either. 'We were bringing nothing home,' Sam says. He and his shipmates pushed past their misgivings to carry on, locked as they were into an economic order built on violence. But an economic order that is not grounded in the ecological order will surely collapse and theirs did.

Today our economically advanced societies are still bulldozing the earth to scoop up its riches, outsourcing suffering to keep our supermarkets stocked while we detach ourselves from the distress. Swept along, watching the world with unease but unable to look it in the eye; a whole life can pass that way, a whole century in Babylon. But it does not have to. All around the world people gather to live out a better story and step out of their suffocating scripts, crying, 'Enough to a lie!' Veterans are joining with conscientious objectors to confront the war system. Land-workers are learning from native peoples how to find a harmonious balance between human needs and the life of the earth. Children and young people are striking from school and blocking the streets for the earth's sake, calling time on an economic system that harms the ground of life itself. Anti-racist movements are right in the face of white silence. Violence bears down and still the pull of life, its promise, is on the move, broadcasting its invitation like seeds. 'You're in a foggy street but you keep going,' says Basma, 'until you feel the lucidity of your life – the numinous feeling of your existence.' Then the choice between love and violence cannot be avoided any longer. Our domesticated script for domesticated success starts to slip its grip. It rips, the tower cracks, the weeds push through.

3. FREEDOM

Hope woken.

Writing about his time as an infantryman in the Falklands War, Ken Lukowiak recalled stumbling across the corpse of a young Argentinian conscript, frozen in the bitter South Atlantic wind. Rifling through the lad's pockets, Ken and his mates find his identity card – he is 17, still a boy. With the card is a small photograph showing the boy outside a house with a woman, likely his mum. 'I thought about how I was to be the first link in the chain that would carry the news of her son's death to her,' Ken wrote. The soldiers pass the photo round, thinking of their own mums who wait helplessly at home.

'Man is still the first weapon of war', according to the military. The primary agents of violence in every place are indeed men, but what marks soldiers out, including the few women who enlist, is that they are weaponised human beings. The army bends the mind of a teenager to a script that requires absolute obedience, trains them to kill on demand, and approves of their violence as a service. The training process is described by military psychologists as 'intense indoctrination'. It begins by isolating new recruits from their family and friends and controlling their behaviour in detail; even a slight deviation is met with punishment and humiliation. Soon the soldier follows every order by reflex but is still not ready to kill. To achieve this the army obscures the humanity of the soldier's opponent, by presenting him as the unkempt, barbaric, anonymous male printed on rifle range target boards. The enemy is never drawn as a woman, or as a 17-year-old conscript, or as anyone like the soldier who shoots the target down. He is presented as a nothing whose death means nothing, but whose killing is a soldier's pride. After a few intense weeks, the army has turned a teenager from Barnsley into a killer by profession, capable of plunging a bayonet into a stranger's heart. And the soldier, if drilled thoroughly enough, will look forward to it; when the news reached Ken's unit that they would be sailing for war in the Falklands, they cheered.

Hope's Work

But now, standing over the punctured corpse of a boy on a windswept hillside eight thousand miles from home, this group of soldiers face a moment of reckoning: their violence has left a mother to bury her son. Which of them can now say that, because the young soldier was a stranger to them, he had no worth? Who can count his own mum of greater worth than the boy's? Who can make the case in honesty that one person should live because he is British and his quest righteous, and another die because he is Argentinian, the enemy of the good? While politicians in both countries watched the killing play out in a map room, in the abstract, with the detachment of spectators, these soldiers snatched a glimpse of the world of a boy they had killed. They felt the worth of human life like a rush and knew then the shame of their violence. Their training had not overcome their humanity after all, it had only smothered it, and here it was pushing back, jolting them awake to the tragedy of war's violence – the wreckage that its calculated, chaotic brutality makes of life.

A hundred thousand similar stories show that traumatic war events, if they are not so overwhelming as to crush the spirit completely, may quicken it in those whose job is to enact the violence. George Zabelka was an American air force chaplain in the Second World War. One morning in August 1945, his job was to reassure the crew of an atomic bomber that they would do God's work that day by burning Nagasaki to the ground with all its children. Afterwards, standing in the city's ruins where a church had once been, he saw the crumpled censer in the ash, and his sin. After a long repentance, he decided to work for peace for the rest of his life.

So did Arthur Galston, after his herbicide was used as a weapon of mass destruction in Vietnam. The American air force released 20 million gallons of the powder, codenamed Agent Orange, to strip forests and fields of their life. Villagers were left to starve; mothers were still giving birth to malformed babies decades later. After the war, Arthur eventually prevailed on his government to outlaw the use of his invention as a weapon.

During the Iraq War, it was Ben Griffin's job as a British 'special forces' soldier to blow holes in people's homes in the small hours of the night. While one of his platoon held the women and children at gunpoint, the others ransacked the house, or bound and hooded the men to be handed over to the Americans to decide their fate. When Ben came home for a mid-tour break, he told the army he would not be going back. Now he tells me that soldiers' hardest memories are not of the violence done to them, but of the violence they have done to others – an observation that the research literature confirms. Their release from the war system can lead into an agonising repentance, first named in the 1980s as 'moral pain', now 'moral injury'. Soldiers among the ranks of ancient Babylon had no name for it, but many of them would have felt just as ill at heart. After the army, Ben founded Veterans for Peace UK, which now tours schools teaching about the true nature of war. The veterans tell children that a soldier is a person that a nation uses for its violence, which begins when they first walk in through the barracks gates and are made to stand in line.

A chaplain said, 'no more'. A scientist said, 'no more'. A soldier said, 'no more'. As witnesses to the reality of war as trauma, each was brought to reckon with his part in it. Each had to face the contradiction between his humanity and his violence; between what he means to be and what he has been made to be. Behind each 'no' is the unheard 'yes' of a humane spirit at work, tearing a hole in the war script, letting the light in.

A violent script may be laid bare in a shocking moment of revelation, but otherwise can function smoothly for decades. Such was the way of the Soviet bloc. Its system of control, which made masterful use of fear to quell all dissent and coerce society into obedience, left the people with no political voice at all. And yet even there the script's grip was not total.

In 1978, a Czechoslovakian dissident predicted that a tide of popular dissent would rise slowly but irresistibly to end his country's suffocating dictatorship. Countless small choices by apparently powerless people, he wrote, each act apparently insignificant by itself, would win them their freedom. He told a parable, which went something like this:

In a greengrocer's window is a patriotic poster, sent to her from the depot with her weekly stock of vegetables; next month a replacement poster arrives, and so on, year after year. Then, one day, she takes it down.

As any of the dissident's readers well knew, posters in shop windows were one of a thousand ways that the Soviet system conjured the illusion that it enjoyed the people's favour. No one would blame a shopkeeper for being made to display one in exchange for a quiet life. But this shopkeeper, one day, refuses. Long having lived a contradiction between what she means to be, and what she has been made to be, she can no longer escape the choice between them. She can either keep playing her part in the oppression of herself and everyone else, or take herself out of it – keep the poster up or take it down.

The essay was titled *The Power of the Powerless* and its author was the playwright Václav Havel. He explained why the shopkeeper's simple choice matters to a politically silenced people: 'In this revolt the greengrocer steps out of living within the lie,' he wrote. In recovering her 'suppressed identity and dignity', her act is 'an attempt to live within the truth' and makes a clear break from the oppressive script she has been made to follow. Taking the poster down seems to achieve nothing but it gives 'concrete significance', Havel believed, to her freedom as a human being, and so it means everything.

No sudden shock jolted the greengrocer into awareness and action, so why does she take the poster down, and why now, on this completely ordinary day? We can imagine, I think, that a long series of faintly troubling moments has been leading her to her to-be-or-not-to-be moment. Perhaps a bit of dissident graffiti makes her think, a crumpled pamphlet makes sense of her doubts, a conversation in the shadows assures her she is not alone. We can picture all these encounters, the pull of life at work in them, tugging at her humanity until the burden of living the Soviet lie weighs so heavily … that the scales tip. And although her choice is lonely, she has never really been alone; all along, a culture of resistance has lived in the cracks in the tower, opening them wider, anticipating the day when the entire edifice of oppression can no longer hold itself up.

Havel's essay was smuggled throughout the Soviet bloc on blue carbon copies. At the Ursus tractor factory in Poland, Zbygniew Bujak had been trying for a long time to mobilise his fellows against the system, getting nowhere. 'Why are we taking such risks?' he wondered. He found an answer in Havel's essay, but not the cliché that truth prevails – that too is a lie. It told him that the alternative to living within the truth is no alternative at all; that a people's struggle in hope for their own destiny, *even when nothing seems to change,* is the expression of their freedom now and an intimation of a larger freedom in waiting. The essay encouraged dissident workers to keep cultivating the kind of character and fellowship that are capable, in the manner of the greengrocer, of stepping out of the dehumanising script of the Soviet bloc. Zbygniew's fellow workers passed the essay round. It kept them going, he said; 'we did not give up, and a year later … the management were afraid of us. We mattered.' Ten years later, all of Czechoslovakia's shopkeepers would tear down their patriotic posters and the people would make Václav Havel the first president of a new republic.

If the Soviet lie was borne as a burden, the Western lie is a comfort to consume. It woos with the self-congratulation of 'this great nation', whichever it happens to be. It whispers listlessly from wall-to-wall adverts, flogging the fleeting satisfactions of every kind of guff. It noises off in press headlines, carefully crafted to indulge the reader's fear of faces that fail to fit. Our script, no less than its Soviet counterpart, works by dispossession and control, as a kind of abstract oppression that locks in the concrete oppression of all the life it pushes to the margins. And although, compared with the Soviet system, we enjoy greater licence to come and go, and to speak up or keep silent, the liberty of having many options is not the freedom of standing in the world as the people we mean to be.

Writer James Baldwin once said that African Americans, because they and their ancestors have suffered, and because they share in faith and the blues, know what they live for, but he doubted the same could be said of America on the whole. He wondered aloud that 'most Americans have been for so long, so safe and sleepy, that they don't any longer have any real sense of what they live by. I think they really think it may be Coca-

Cola.' After the Ku Klux Klan bombed an Alabama church killing four children, James Baldwin would not condemn white people as a whole, but he did condemn the safe and sleepy silence of white America which, knee on the neck of black America, then and now, just keeps calm and carries on.

The same white, patriarchal, consumer culture now shapes the world, not least my childhood town, Stratford-upon-Avon. The town serves as a kind of economically walled-in haven for an affluent few, whose windows it was my dad's living to clean. Today, when I walk past the *Miracle-Gro* lawns and parked-up four-by-fours, how 'safe and sleepy' the town seems, how silently untroubled by the world beyond its green and pleasant horizon. For me, it has become a place of *solastalgia* – that experience of homesickness you can get without even leaving home. I could not feel further away from the bluesy, faithful, deeply hopeful practices of black survival and vitality that James Baldwin knew with such passion and pain. But no sudden jolt to the system seems to be on its way; no dissident graffiti can yet be found; no subversive pamphlet is moving from hand to hand in the shadows. What on earth,

I wonder, promises to interrupt and upset this false peace, except perhaps the end of the world?

Every day on my way to school I crossed the river past the Shakespeare theatre, not once going in. Since my school allowed its students to opt out of English literature completely and I did, I was well into adulthood before I saw a Shakespeare play. Finally, for a £10 standing ticket – a value exactly equivalent to the penny cost of standing as a *groundling* for a play in Shakespeare's day – I met his radicalising dreams for the first time.

In *As You Like It* I felt I had found a parable for my hometown. Like other Shakespeare plays, this one feeds its well-heeled audience in the gallery with a pleasing tale, while smuggling a more unsettling story to the *groundlings* at the foot of the stage. On the surface, the play is a kind of aristo romcom caper, which moves by wit and wonder from its beginning in a dreary palace towards an exuberantly joyful ending in a forest. Behind the fun and games, Shakespeare lays open the vanity and cruelty of the monied class of his day and ours; those few who relentlessly dispossess the many. Shakespeare's setting is Stratford's local forest, the

Arden, which when the play was written in 1599 had become asylum to hundreds of poor families kicked off their land by the wealthy.

Among the play's subversive strands is its story of two brothers: dukes, men who are used to living in comfort and sending soldiers to war to keep things that way. For a long time, the older duke has presided over his realm as the well-meaning overlord; perhaps he cherishes liberal values, takes intelligent newspapers, and discusses the plight of the poor over fine wine. But his infatuation with the comforts of his class has turned him tame, so the playwright sends in the jealous younger duke, who seizes the palace and banishes his brother to the forest with his courtiers in tow, and so the drama begins.

We follow the old duke and his exiled court into the Arden. To these pampered aristocrats, the woods seem a 'desert place' of fear and boredom, devoid of meaning. But as the seasons turn, the duke and his company grow ragged and the forest comes slowly alive to them, until everywhere are 'tongues in trees, books in the running brooks, sermons in stones'. A wild spell is upon them, breaking them down and setting them free from their dull, oppressive scripts, even as the play's romcom plot romps on. Winter cuts deep, says the dishevelled old duke at last, but its hardships now 'feelingly persuade me what I am'.

For a while, the duke and his tattered company live like 'the old Robin Hood', as one of the characters dares to declare. This is not the Robin Hood of Hollywood, but the legendary folk outlaw remembered from the medieval tavern song, who from his forest home takes on the power of the city, outwitting the corrupt and doling out their comeuppance. In Shakespeare's time, Robin's persona would also lead the joyfully anarchistic May games in parishes up and down the country despite their harsh suppression by Church and Crown. Here on the stage Shakespeare brings the same, subversive spring carnival to life again, right under the noses of the royal censors.

While the play's main characters exchange the sighs of young love, Shakespeare is slowly turning the violent social order upside down. The old duke and his company, through their encounters in the forest, are challenged to share their food with the hungry, to 'mend' the wages of a farmsteader dispossessed, and to learn the worth of the foresters' lives for the first time. In a throwaway line, Shakespeare has the hungry duke hurl a final insult against the aristocrat class by poaching deer from Arden's local lord. Poaching was a desperate act of survival for many in the late 1500s, but also the most symbolically potent – and personally risky – direct action against the land-grabbing injustices of the wealthy.

All told, the duke is still a creature of civilisation and this play is still a romance looking for its happily-ever-after. In the end the spell breaks, Shakespeare restores the duke to his former power, and the play closes. What happens next? Defying the real-world aristocracy of 1599, Shakespeare's duke promises to share his 'returned fortune' with everyone he has met in the forest. Or perhaps, back on his throne, he will lapse into the empty luxury he knew before: the half-eaten banquets and lavish trips to distant lands that an aristocrat takes to be their entitlement. But if his trial in the forest has had any grace to it at all, something of it will travel home with him. Perhaps he will seem oddly shabby under his crown, not quite the part, shaken, a little more generous than is usual for such a man of power.

All that as it may be, it is the younger, upstart duke's story that I suspect a Black liberationist such as James Baldwin would most want us to heed. Having kicked his brother off his throne in the first act, the young duke enjoys all the worldly power he ever dreamed of: a bigger carriage, a bigger palace, a bigger army, a bigger pile of gold. By the norms of his day and ours he has won life's game, but he paces up and down his palace, listless and lonely. Even the play ignores him until the very end, when he ventures out to witness his brother's happiness in the forest, but he halts at the threshold. Imagine that: a man of worldly dominion peering into the half-light of the wildwood – or a juke joint, or a Harlem church – and feeling the pull of its life but fearing to go in. There the young duke stands, stuck between the suffocating comforts of the palace behind him – or his suburban mansion with excellent links to the city – and, in front of him, the frightening, vivifying, who-knows-what of a world wilder than he can bear. Eventually, an 'old religious man' stops to hear his story and the young aristocrat is 'converted from the world' to become a monk. When he abandons his crown for his older brother to find, it is with relief.

If we, the audience, can remember the play not only as a skilled performance, but as a dream we have just lived, then perhaps, like the old duke, something of our time in the forest will travel home with us. In setting the palace as a comfortable, controlled, well-defended, and finally lifeless place where people are 'merely players', Shakespeare has laid bare the privileges of indulgent wealth and called the high dream of civilisation into question. We have been invited instead into the greenwood as a living, breathing place of seasonal metamorphosis, whose natural abundance stands at odds with worldly wealth. Unlike the wilderness that undoes humanity in other stories such as *Lord of the Flies*, here the forest gathers the players in, breaks them down, draws forth who they really are, turns them around, and then lets them go on their way. May it also be so for us. Here again is nature's extraordinarily hopeful work, blowing through a long-dead playwright whose radical imagination is still completely alive today.

A soldier is so shamed by his violence that he refuses to re-join the war. A shopkeeper on a street of shopkeepers stops playing the game that holds her people to ransom. A young man seizes his brother's wealth only to give it up. Truth breaks through their scripts, beckoning them to a larger freedom. And that means, first, to be thrown out of kilter – to become confused – until a pivotal choice is faced between the old way and the new.

People who, like me, have been socialised into the stagnant dreams of a white, Western, middle-class cultural world have no Shakespeare to decant us magically into exile, dispossess us of the comforts of domestication, reenchant us with the wildness we have lost, and send us back, ready to begin again. Yet sometimes, reality breaks in to reveal the many forms of violence that preserve us as an economically over-comfortable class. In *As You Like It* this is the forest's doing. In *The Tempest*, enslaved Caliban delivers the same wild upset to the civilised order. The forest did it again in the biblical story of Daniel, where Nebuchadnezzar, Babylon's hard-hearted king, is exiled to live as an animal until his 'body was drenched with the dew of heaven'. It is the evergreen work of the wild tricksters of myth and legend – Robin Hood certainly, but also Enkidu, Merlin, and Pan – and of the healer women feared by patriarchs as 'witches' in every age. Their gift to us is to tip the comfortable imperium up: to *humble*, literally bring us 'back to earth', and so feelingly persuade us of what we really are.

4. DISILLUSION

Hope threshed.

Around Nelson's Column and boxed-in *Eros*, past the palace guard and Liberty's bolted glass doors, a million people moved. On one grey day in 2003, we rose like a river in spate, massive and slow, bursting our banks, to say no.

But the government, its military, and big business were set on following the world's superpower into a one-sided invasion of Iraq, whose dictator had outlived his uses. The prime minister dismissed our march with a wave of the hand, saying we did not understand the world as he did. Media barons cheered him on. Parliament approved the war as democratic. Tens of thousands of missiles pulverised Iraq from above, then thousands of tanks buried its conscript armies in the desert. The American general said he would not be counting the dead. After six weeks, the victory bugle sounded over a bombed-out shell of a country. But, with corruption in its government, Western armies bogged down in its cities, warlords amok in the hinterland, and Islamist extremists surging in with plans for a total takeover, Iraq was pushed into chaos. More than a decade after the war's 'end', the country is one of the most violent places on earth. From time to time the politicians and generals pass the blame around, but now the oil is flowing their way once more, from the old Babylon to the new.

In national memory, 15 February 2003 has become the day the people said no to war: civilisation was losing its head; democracy itself was at stake; a distant country was under threat; it was time for solidarity against a superpower thug and this time we would make our leaders listen. But we were not as good as all that. Most people in Britain remember opposing the war from the start, according to surveys taken a decade afterwards, but at the time the majority were, in fact, ready to support war if it was approved as lawful. When it began without that approval most people supported it anyway. A minority had been opposed to the invasion throughout, but only a handful did much about it either before the big march or afterwards. 'The masses are always on the verge of becoming something totally different from what they seem to be,' wrote Rosa Luxemburg, but this time we went home from our march pretty much the same as we turned up to it. If the people were a new global superpower, it lasted a day.

Many marchers still look back on our protest as a waste of time. Some say we could have stopped the war if only there had been more of us, or if instead of marching from A to B we had joined the few activists busy disrupting military bases. But this is a big 'if only'. It assumes no gap between what we could do and what we are willing to do. It imagines a liberal public, optimistic for a better world but baulking at the cost, to become a radical public, pessimistic but ready to put itself on the line. As things turned out, we achieved 'absolutely nothing', according to one of the organisers.

In search of someone to blame, we have remembered a prime minister far too sure of himself, but we might also remember that the rush to take over other countries has been one of Britain's oldest habits. This or that leader's character aside, war has been, in ancient

Babylon as today, the natural and predictable outcome of a deadly game of power primed for violence. Its strongest players lie awake at night wondering not how to end the harm, but how to turn it to advantage. As the first global superpower, Britain invaded and colonised most countries in the world. Now, in fear of irrelevance, it has been jumping to join the latest superpower in its every war of choice. Such is post-imperial Britain's somewhat desperate hope of preserving a sense of self-worth, which for centuries has been pegged to a sense of global importance.

This, at any rate, is the view that I have reached after my own years of campaigning. When I started, my hopes were high but shallow-rooted. I told my friends I wanted to help develop peace processes, as if war were merely a tragic problem in a faraway land that waited for a technical solution from a white peace dove like me. I still believe that peace – not merely the absence of violence but the presence of right relationship at every level, the dignity of our common being – is as real as violence. But peace is also a struggle through a traumatised landscape dominated by rogue superpowers, corporations, media conglomerates, and military generals who say they abhor war but are first to push for it. None among these pauses to read our placards. From the high towers of Babylon old and new, history's rulers have looked down on the crowds below as naïve. To them, we have seemed as indifferent to the world beyond our immediate horizons as we are incapable of grasping its complexity; our dissent is at best a problem to be managed, at worst just an irritant to be salved. We are the 'mob', from *mobile vulgus* meaning fickle crowd, a term coined nearly 400 years ago by British aristocrats to ridicule the rising influence of people power. Their social heirs of 2003 were just as dismissive, sneering in the press at the 'futile commotion' of our 'All Fools' Day' protest.

No wonder that many marchers were left disillusioned, but disillusion – the sweeping away of illusions – is hope's vital pain. If hope is to be more than just another way of hiding from the world as a tragic place, it must first be free of the hocus-pocus promises of redemption that shape the politics of our times. Of all our false hopes, the inhumane kind seem to be on the rise, such as the expectation that high walls, big guns, periodic purges, and a self-willed strongman will bludgeon a better future into being. Other hopes have a magical air; the assumption that poverty and war are part of a divine plan is common to millions of people who believe we should let violence rage on until a god comes to rescue us. Some assumptions, though widely held, are just fake: that the leader with the best jokes will know what to do, or maybe the man with the right kind of suit, or should it be the woman with the finest legs? Other hopes, common among the marchers, are reasonable but just too flimsy: that people can be relied on to care for one another; that when we speak with one voice we are heard; that in a democracy the people own the ship, which has a noble mission but just needs a new captain. Such liberal-democratic ideals, unless they can reckon with abusive power, cannot bear much weight in the work of hope.

We do not give up our illusions; experience wrenches them away. To witness violence of all kinds is to have one's faith in the world shaken and threshed; high hopes without deep roots are blown over. Martin Luther King, after years of fear and doubt, and harbouring daily the foreboding that white violence was coming for him, told his friends one night: 'We have experiences when the light of day vanishes, leaving us in some dark and desolate midnight – moments when our highest hopes are turned into shambles of despair ...' It is as if 'darkness [has] engulfed the earth', and yet, he said, looking at the horizon, there in the east the moon is rising. He points, I think, to the hidden light that the darkness does not snuff out, but instead reveals. This is the moment when we may know, finally, what is genuinely worth believing in.

Or – might Albert Camus be right to suspect that once the last false hope falls away, nothing is left to believe in at all? What if hope is just an elaborate denial of the unthinkable truth that we are doomed? I, for one, have no answer, but this is the point: hope is something we do, not because we know the future, but because we do not know it. It has never been necessary to know the future to meet it well. A world in which we knew exactly what was coming over the horizon could not know the word 'hope'. In his memoir of Auschwitz, Primo Levi described how the total violence of the death camp left the people within its walls 'crushed against the bottom' of existence. At the same time, he felt inexplicably possessed by a 'senseless, crazy residue of unavoidable hope'. The possibility of happiness had died, and yet it was impossible, he wrote, to allow the possibility of happiness to die – not because he knew he would survive, but precisely because he did not know.

It is possible that events bring such abject disillusion that all hope fails, but any hopes that experience does not strip away are exactly that: the ones we cannot get rid of. Once all the chaff is threshed away, real hopes remain like a few grains in the hand. These are unlikely, I think, to include a deepened faith in liberal democracy, still less any kind of gunboat autocracy or fascistic design. The hopes that endure will be simpler, more surprising, and more vital than these, and not as tidily reassuring. For the imprisoned Mansur, for example, what stayed with him was the sun rising each morning. Just imagine: you are asked what gives you hope and all you say – all you need to say – is, 'The earth is alive.'

The cover of this book shows *Victory Palm*, an engraving made by Emily Johns in 2008. The work remembers a day when American planes dropped 40,000 pounds of bombs on the date groves that line the road running out of Baghdad towards the ruins of ancient Babylon. Its title recalls that the date is a sacred symbol of life and health, with which Muslims end their fast each day during Ramadan, and that a palm frond was an offering to congratulate a military success in antiquity. The broken palms that fill the image are like 'cut-down people', says Emily, after the painting *Menin Road* by Paul Nash, in which shredded trees dominate the desolate fields of Flanders after the First World War.

In the near corner of this violated landscape, a lone prisoner stands. Though bound and blindfolded, he stands not as victim but as witness to the life that has been lost and that remains: the few trees that are still alive. 'Bold' is Emily's word for him. The moon, keeper of time since before the days of Marduk, throws light upon the man as if it bears witness also, and has not given up on him just yet. *Victory Palm*, like much of Emily's artwork, is unusual in holding despair and hope together in the same image, without flinching. I ask her all the same how this work, showing the aftermath of devastating violence, can still speak of hope: 'It's a matter of dignity,' she says, with the prisoner in mind. Rather like Mansur, he has lost almost everything, but not the dignity of knowing who he is and what he loves.

Writer Natalia Ginzburg is another who once had everything wrenched away. After her home was bombed to bits in the Second World War, her faith in the world was left shaken for a long time.

Because so much that she loved had been taken from her once, she knew it could be taken again – it was no longer safe for her to rely on even the solid bricks and mortar of her new home:

> 'True, we have a lamp on the table again, and a little vase of flowers, and pictures of our loved ones, but we can no longer trust any of these things because once, suddenly, we had to leave them behind, or because we have searched through the rubble for them in vain.'

The war seemed to give Natalia a special, uncomfortable knowledge of the fragility of the things that most of us assume to be solid, sound. But the war failed, even at the height of its clamour, to rob her or her people of certain essentials: '[P]erhaps this is the one good thing that has come out of the war. Not to lie, and not to allow others to lie to us.'

For ecologist Ashlee Cunsolo, disillusion began in childhood, when an unexpected act of violence provoked such a surge of humane feeling in her that it transformed her worldview:

Disillusion

'When I was five, a pond and thicket area down the street from my house was filled in and levelled while I was away ... denuded of all greenery, and completely empty of the beavers and their dam, the minnows, the birds, and the countless rabbits and squirrels ... [I was] consumed and overcome by grief and loss. I did not want to eat, or play, or go to school ...'

While most of the adults in Ashlee's life shrugged that this was just the way the world works, she mourned the loss. And she shed a child's illusion – wholly reasonable but wholly wrong – that nature's living home carries such grace that no one would want to violate it. A wrecking ball crashed through her world yet left her with vital knowledge: that the peace of living things is ever vulnerable before civilisation.

'It was the first time in my short life that I became aware of the fragility of life – mine and others – and from that moment, I found myself in a different life-world full of the awareness of the potential for death and injury to befall plants, animals, and ecosystems ...'

And the same life urges the commitments of love:

> '[T]hose early days of grief and sadness created the foundations for my personal acts and responses to mourning – acts and responses that grew and transformed with each subsequent loss, with each grief process, with each work of mourning I undertook.'

The arc of all these testimonies moves through the grief of disillusion towards a kind of hope that we could call *conscious*, in both senses: 'aware' and 'meant'. Natalia and Ashlee, as well as Basma, Mansur, George Zabelka, even Václav Havel's dissident shopkeeper, all carry the wounds of their experience. And with their scars they carry the imperatives of a well-threshed hope: remember your dignity, tell the truth, mourn the losses, know that life is vulnerable, and keep loving it – it matters. The meaning of being human and of hope become one, in a kind of charged existence: alive in freedom and love, off-script, and on the move.

Our stop-the-war march did not seem to turn many of us towards new meaning, but we had gathered around a common feeling that, as a society, we were falling short of what we meant to be. If the march was not one of conscious hope, it was at least one of disaffection – the anguish that comes when we and our world seem to be moving apart. Our disaffection rose in a flood that day. However fickle, ignorant, self-centred, or confused the political class imagined our mob to be, our disaffection had more life in it than their bleached-bones narrative of 'global order', 'regime change', and 'strategic outcomes'. And muddled though our motives often were, our disaffection bore witness to all the harm that was and still is ours to answer for.

At dusk, the waters abated, the silt of our protest sank into the ground, but the work of that day was not yet done. Seeds of dissent would soon take root to unsettle the architects of the invasion, whose lofty dismissal of the march had shown that they were prepared to ignore the people to preserve their own power. The disastrous war to come exposed the gang violence of Western nations as self-appointed leaders of the world. The march and its aftermath helped to bring us, the public, into clearer consciousness of our condition, to shift the ground on which our politics is made, and to make a reckless rush to war a little less likely in years to come. While the Queen's Christmas message of that year quietly passed over the country's largest ever public protest, a decade later the UK's military chief admitted that public opposition to war had become one of his greatest worries about the future. By such measures as these, that day was worth every shuffling footstep.

But soon, the children of Iraq would be burning in the fireballs of bombs made in Stevenage by people who tuck their own children into bed each night. Disaffection alone is not enough, and a march is not a revolution.

5. FELLOWSHIP

Hope shared.

An old man, out with his granddaughters for a spring walk on the lakeshore, lifts the end of a rock and scoops up a frog for the children to see. They flinch at the creature's glistening angles and outrageous eyes, but they are also rapt and drawn in. They want to touch it, explore it, and they hesitate – might they hurt it? – but granddad nods. The old man looks on as their fingers explore the animal gently. I watch from a distance. His silence seems to say: *This is yours. But not like a possession is yours.* He might as well be holding the whole earth in his palm.

The frog's uncanny stillness leads the children in a sort of dance. It repels them, invites them, enchants them, and leaves them finally with this: *Take care.* The earth is involved, too, as the old man's co-conspirator in bringing the children to this encounter with the vitality of their world. Its *viriditas* – its wild, 'green truth' – saturates the moment. Right now, the children know that the frog and its living home deserve their attention, which is their love, and they want no harm.

I wonder at the long journey these children have before them. Will they turn from nature as wild wonder in favour of some tame fantasy of a tidier world? Will the unsettling majesty of a frog shrink away to nothing but a sack of warts that stones were meant to hide? Maybe. But the time that granddad gives them now will count for something. If the children remember themselves, if they are well-loved in their own love of the life in and around them, and if they can bear all that has yet to deluge them in their passage through adolescence to adulthood, then the charge of humane vitality that infuses them today stands every chance of guiding their lives tomorrow. Granddad is doing a little of hope's work, holding it out in his hand and passing it on.

Childhood was also when Alice Walker's journey in hope began to stir, wowed by the crazy circus of creepy-crawlies in the ground: '… I connected very early with the feeling that the earth is alive. If you're down there crawling around, you soon realised that it's teeming with beings.'

Fellowship

Hands at her keyboard, Alice Walker has been reminding us over and over, as if to say, *Look! Life is here, take care*. Writing on the sexist and racist violence of America, she draws life's tragedy closely; her stories are immersed in it. But she draws out life's promise, too, in characters who have to work at holding faith with their love. That promise may be slight, found in flecks of the purple wildflowers that dance in the windy share-croppers' fields. The flowers are sparse, fleeting, but alive, undeniable, busy wooing Alice's characters and her readers, tilting them towards the knowledge that life is worth its work.

In the years when the young Alice Walker was grubbing about in the soil, Ann Druyan and Carl Sagan were poring over the night sky, 'a place so strange and desolate that, by comparison, planets and stars and galaxies seem achingly rare and lovely'. Preoccupied with exposing the folly of the Cold War, the two scientists believed that the natural experience of wonder could humble and humanise, such that the nuclear rivalry of the superpowers would be embarrassed as the petty hubris it was. Together they made America's most-watched documentary series, *Cosmos*, as an ode to the immense, ancient architecture of all that is. Somewhere in that vastness, they wrote, 'we float like a mote of dust in the morning sky' – and are still, 'in some pain and with no guarantees, working out our destiny'. They appealed to us to know that we inhabit a life-giving mystery that is inviting us in, on which the entire human journey could yet pivot. Away from the lab and the TV studio, Ann and Carl would join hands with hundreds of others at sit-ins on nuclear bases in the Nevada desert, confronting the life-denying violence of their times.

Meanwhile, Helen Steven was confronting the nuclear system in Scotland. Bolt-cutter in hand, she cut through its weldmesh fences, then told her court hearing why: 'This beautiful, delicate world in all its infinite wonder is threatened with extinction. That to me is blasphemy.' For Helen, violence was more than an injury to humanity, but a sacrilegious offence – theft from the stock of the world's promise. With an all-colour sensibility for the sacred worth of living things, she embarrassed the monochrome fantasy of the nuclear planners: men in suits playing at war in their heads, chalking up cities for annihilation as 'assets held at risk', calculating the 'probabilities of penetration' of a 'pre-emptive first strike'. Helen's work and words confronted such lifeless war talk with the humanity that it cannot cope with.

These are stories of people who, moved by the life around them, try to meet it with their own. Each holds faith with the perfect worth of humanity and the earth, vulnerable as it is before civilised violence, and invites love for what deserves to be loved. Each testifies to the slenderness of hope's action, but also to its relentless movement through the world. And each reveals the difference between being a witness, involved intimately in the world as place of vitality, and a spectator, who merely looks out on the world, detached, from a distance. From a childhood encounter with amphibian fragility to a courtroom speech on the blasphemy of violence, these are stories of encounters where hope unfurls its perennial appeal to all of us. And as hope is received and passed on in fellowship, the 'weave of relation' that can 'hold strong' in the face of violence, as community worker Lisa Cumming has put it, is packed tighter.

In hope's fellowship, everyone has a place. Not all of us are willing to break into nuclear bases before dawn, but those who are will be needing breakfast; the people who cook it for them take their own place in hope's work. The hands that cut the fence and the hands that chop the onions could be anybody's, as could the hands that hold a fragile creature so that children may know it for what it is. And the hands of a harried mum or dad who somehow still find the time to play with their children, and hands that plant trees or dress wounds, and musicians' hands, whose work restores us for tomorrow. All hands can take a little of the work and so participate hope's ecology, the life by which it lives. It will not always feel like it, said the activist Joyce Pickard, but to be part of the work is a privilege; we just need to know what share of hope's work is our own to hold.

Such a fellowship of hope may be the only force vital enough to face violence down. Monica Coleman, a minister and theologian, writes about a group of African-American women who have been abused by their partners and meet each week to support one another:

'On this particular evening … we were braiding down the patches of Lisa's hair so that we could fit her for a wig. Earlier that day, Lisa's boyfriend had pulled her around the apartment by her hair, dragging her limp and battered body behind him. This left bald patches all over her scalp, as her hair had literally been ripped from her head in handfuls … I held the right side of her head with the palm of my hand. Her entire body quivered, and this made the task of braiding all the more difficult. The other women in the group were quiet as they gently rubbed Lisa's shoulders or leg to assure her of their sympathetic presence: *Yeah, girl, we know*. Many of them did … Who else could understand that hair was not trivial for black women? We knew that Lisa would not feel strong enough or woman enough to go to work, confront her boyfriend, or be seen anywhere in public as long as her hair looked like this. But Lisa was still crying as we were pulling tiny pieces of hair into small plaits, working around the bald spots.'

It is hard to imagine, particularly for me as a white man, what it is like for these women to leave the group for the night and face violence in their own homes. By Monica's account, their fellowship offers something of the solidarity – the 'weave of relation' – that they need to hold strong.

When one woman is knocked down, the others bear her up and hold her woundedness with her; she draws on their hope to recover her own. By braiding down Lisa's hair, the women show not only that they care about her, but also that they believe in her. Their attentive, quiet presence invites Lisa back to herself, as a woman with a woman's dignity. As the women hold their wounds in common, so it seems they hold their hope in common, the touch of their hands doing hope's impatiently patient work.

'In the collective vulnerability of presence, we learn not to be afraid,' writes Alice Walker. Or perhaps the most we learn is to be less afraid, which can yet be enough to make the difference between hope and no hope. The presence of others seems so essential to holding hope in the face of violence, that we might wonder how a lonely hopefulness can possibly endure. So many stories do tell of a lonely path: individuals who step out on their own. On one night a week, Lisa can lean on the fellowship of her group, but how lonely does the journey home become for her?

And yet, even when the fellowship of hope seems absent, might it still be present? People who step out in hope speak again and again about the solidarity of those who accompany them, even when they are entirely exiled from friends and allies. For decades, Israel's secret police – the Shabak – has captured, isolated, and tortured Palestinian dissidents to get them to produce confessions. Like all institutions of its kind, the Shabak is afraid to call its violence by its name, so it refers to its torture as 'special methods', which were routine until the late 1990s and still continue today. Interrogators have bound their captives' limbs, beaten them, and thrown them in cells no bigger than a coffin to induce claustrophobia. But the defenceless prisoners are not, in fact, defenceless; many have learned mental resistance techniques inspired by Julius Fučík, a Czech dissident captured and tortured by the Gestapo in the Second World War, whose secret writings made their way around the world. In one technique, a captive under torture will imagine themselves at home with comrades and family, especially their mother. The academic Lena Meari has spent time with Palestinian dissidents to hear their stories, among them this testimony from a detainee named Marshud:

'While chained and tied in a distorted and extremely painful position in the closet [a cell no bigger than the person it holds], I was walking around my city of Ramallah, accompanied by my comrades, family, and beloved. I was envisioning how I would be received by them when released without providing a confession.'

By intensifying the duress, the Shabak could sometimes extract the information it wanted, but not when those like Marshud turned their willingness to die into a potent force against their jailers. Some did die, refusing to the end to break faith with the people they loved and the cause they shared. And yet this has only made the dissidents more powerful; Marshud and his comrades became stories of hope, which have been broadcast across Palestine like so many seeds on the wind and which the Shabak has neither the imagination nor the strength to chase down.

In a domestic abuse support group in America, as among the dissident captives of Israel's jails, hope is sustained collectively in the fellowship of friends and allies who come together, in the memory of them when they are absent, and in their stories after they are gone. Some people of hope will find the same alliance in the teeming earth as it fills every tiny niche with all the life it can muster.

And what might God have to do with hope? Absolutely nothing, according to millions of nonreligious people who show clearly enough that the love and freedom driving humane choices can prosper without any belief in a God. And absolutely everything, according to those of us who allow the unquantifiable possibility that a God, whatever God is, animates the life by which hope moves – a God that, in spite of who we are, because of who we are, believes in all of us against the odds. When an old man holds in his hand a frog for his grandchildren to see, it is just a frog. This is simply true, and it is enough. But, to paraphrase the medieval theologian Julian of Norwich, it is also true that by some power it is made, by some power it is loved, and by some power it is preserved. Who can say what that power is, be it God or not God, but who could deny that it *is*? Whatever its true name, it seems, in a mystery befitting a mysterious universe, to *conspire* with us – literally 'breathe with us' – in the work of hope.

6. FAITH

Hope tested.

The children are sleeping when the monster comes for them. Sirens and floodlights invade their bedrooms. Mum and dad are carrying the family out the door, but the bulldozer is already here, flanked by tanks and soldiers, so they bundle out the back and huddle together while their home is ripped down.

The bulldozer is the armoured attack-dog of a colonial power, which has robbed a people of its homeland and now suppresses all resistance. The machine's only job is to raze houses to the ground – sometimes to make way for new colonists, sometimes just to punish the families of local dissidents. Tonight, it hunts for tunnels, which people here have dug to break the siege laid against them in their own land.

The Irish activist Eóin Murray arrives at the scene in the morning:

'We were standing in the rubble of a [man's] home ... Around us were the fragments of his life: papers flapping in the wind, a crushed fridge surrounded by grey concrete blocks with metal poles protruding. Children played in the rubble while nearby a group of women lit a fire and huddled close ... Everything this man once had was gone: his home, his clothes, family memorabilia, children's toys, his ID cards and paperwork ...'

Eóin continues:

'[A] small boy, perhaps eight years old, arrived along with a metal tray. On it were small glasses full of tea, short porcelain cups of cardamom-infused coffee and a small white plate piled with pita bread ... A smile opened on [the man's] face and he said, "You are guests of ours, please eat and drink."'

This is Gaza. Last night's violence was just one movement of one cog in the machinery of the Israeli state. Having evicted a million Palestinians from their homeland in 1948, the Israeli military has kept its knee on the Palestinian neck ever since. Aided by America's money and weapons, abetted by a British blind eye, houses are still being demolished today, villages levelled.

In 2014, Israel's 51-day invasion of Gaza killed more than two thousand people. The UN reported a catalogue of war crimes: more than a third of the dead were children, a quarter of whom were blown up in their sleep; a further thousand kids were permanently disabled, and more than that were left orphaned. Rockets fired in retaliation by Palestinian militants killed six people, including a child – also a war crime. At the time of writing, for a year Palestinians in Gaza have gathered in their hundreds at the fence that cages them in to protest their brutal and unambiguously unlawful treatment. Israel's military snipers have picked off the protesters, killing 267 people including 50 children to date, apparently using American bullets made more lethal by a special design that causes them to mushroom when they enter the body. Long prevented by Israel from acting on their legal right to return to their homeland, Palestinians now form the largest refugee population in the world. Those who remain in Gaza and the West Bank are a walled-out people in their own land. Those who live in Israel itself are denied the same rights as their Jewish neighbours because, so its prime minister says, 'Israel is the nation state of the Jewish people – and only it.'

Palestine's story seldom reaches our news channels, which devote more time to Westminster village gossip than events over the horizon. When Palestine gets its 60-second segment, its story can seem a confused clamour, a senseless spat somewhere else. Over here, the distant observer is tempted to sigh that it is 'all very complicated' and turn away, like a spectator grown tired of a show that has gone on too long. One glance at the facts on the ground – Israel's 400-mile apartheid wall, its military supremacy crowned with an American blessing, and its vow never to allow Palestinians the same rights as Israeli Jews – leads quickly to the tidy conclusion that the situation is hopeless.

Untidily for us, this is not how most Palestinians see the matter. The man standing in the ruins of his home is not defeated, for the simple reason that he has not forgotten who he is. Despite all that has befallen him, he insists on continuing to be himself, offering hospitality to his guests while a group of women get a fire going in the rubble. 'Please eat and drink.' This triumph of kindness over calamity is profoundly political; it ensures that whatever territory the occupiers occupy, the hearts and minds of these Palestinians have yet to be invaded. There may be little optimism here, but there is nothing hopeless; these are people working hard today to keep their tomorrow alive.

Palestinians have a word for this: *sumud*. Meaning 'steadfastness' in Arabic, it is used by Palestinians to mean something like holding faith with who they are. *Sumud* is like a fire kept burning through a long night. They see by it, live by it, take comfort from it, refuse to be defined by the darkness of their occupiers' colonial order. *Sumud* is a bond of solidarity, the shared conviction of a whole society that the cause of liberation is the duty of everyone. At its heart is the land: 'not the space where you live,' says the cook Mirna Bamieh, 'but the place where you practise your being as a human being, as a Palestinian, as a culture, as a lineage of ancestors.'

In a common *sumud* practice, exiled Palestinian families pass the housekey from their former home down the generations. Odd though it might seem to treasure a key to a demolished house, it symbolises a future of restitution that waits to be unlocked. In the mind the prospect of returning home is an idea, but in the key it also has a shape and feel – the family's hope is placed in the hands of a child, who holds it in trust. In this and other ways, *sumud* is made real in the things people have and do, where every cherished object and ritual practice reaches for the future but has its roots in the present, in the gathering of people and their longing for the land that is theirs.

Palestinian art represents *sumud* as the olive tree. Whereas for Christians, Jews, and Muslims, the olive's promise is carried in its branches, Palestinians also find meaning in the roots, which push deep into the thinnest of soils to live for hundreds of years, even through drought. In the land of miracles, this must be one of its greatest: that a living thing can turn dusty earth into oily fruit using only the sun and a little rain, and so fulfil the natural promise of the earth. In their bid to disrupt Palestinian society, Israeli colonists and the military have killed half a million olive trees since the turn of the millennium, reversing centuries of cultivation and bringing ruin to Palestinian farmers. Palestinians are as familiar with the upturned tree as they are with the annual olive harvest, but today the roots of their *sumud* are firm still.

In some contrast to Palestine, Western societies commodify land as 'real estate' and homes as 'properties', words more preoccupied with what to possess than how to belong. A culturally mainstream Western imagination will struggle with the idea of *sumud* as the determination to be a free people living in and from their land. But working its way through the rips in our script, something like *sumud* has always been on the move in our own traditions of hopeful dissent.

Seventeenth-century England was in certain ways like Palestine today. The gentry and aristocracy, with the Church's blessing, had long since dispossessed the poor of their land and turned it to their own profit. The smallholders, thrown off the land they called home, were forced to hire out their labour, when they were worked to the bone and bled dry through tithes and taxes. When civil war tore through Britain, and after successive failed harvests had left tens of thousands starving, a few small groups started to push back.

On All Fools' Day in the year 1649, a motley clutch of folk turned up on a Surrey heathland named after that dragon-killer, Saint George, to plant carrots and beans. They pitched tents and began to work and eat together. They came to be known as the Diggers. Their leader, Gerrard Winstanley, declared their belief, much as Palestinians do today using other words, that true religion is 'to make restitution of the Earth, which hath been taken and held from the Common people'. An official report at the time described their activities:

'[W]hat they did was to renew the ancient Community of the enjoying of fruits of the Earth and to distribute the benefit thereof to the Poore and needy, and to feed the Hungry, and to cloathe the Naked ... And for those that will come in and worke [i.e. join them], they shall have meat, drinke and clothes, which is all that is necessary for the life of man; and that for money, there was not any need of it, nor of any clothes more then to cover their nakednesse. And that they will not defend themselves by Armes ...'

Here in the Diggers was something like the fire of Palestinian *sumud*: a determination to push back against a system of coercion and control, simply to be the people they were in their own homeland. They offended the local lord's fantasy of a tidy world; they were 'disorderly and tumultuous', he complained, and he mocked their cause as 'ridiculous'. The Diggers replied that they were only acting for their freedom, asking 'whether the earth with her fruits, was made to be bought and sold from one to another'. In scenes that Palestinians would find familiar today, local thugs and the military tore down the Diggers' tents and ripped up their crops. No one fought back; Winstanley wrote that the Diggers' way was 'Love and Patience ... or else we count it no Freedom'. They just put their tents back up and sowed anew. Other makeshift community farms sprang up and quickly became the talk of the country.

The elite of the day did not like this at all. They looked down on the

Diggers as barbarians, heathens, a threat to civilised society. A year after the first sowing at St George's Hill, a local clergyman brought fifty men to burn their camp down in God's name. When he turned for home, the now-homeless families with their children were left to sleep that April night on the hillside. This final, total act of violence cut short the Diggers' chapter in England's history, but they had done what they meant to do: to love their 'Mother the earth' and their God, who after all had 'made the Earth to be a Common Treasury' for everyone to enjoy. Winstanley wrote finally: 'I have Acted, I have Peace.' It was now time to 'wait to see the Spirit do his own work in the hearts of others'.

And that spirit is indeed astir. The same feeling for the world's promise and determination to face its tragedy have always gathered people into movements like so many streams and rivers running through every continent and age. In India, something like *sumud* is born as *satyagraha*, the power of truthfulness, and in Latin America as *firmeza permanente*, relentless insistence; in southern African peoples it appears again as *ubuntu*, of which one meaning is a shared faith in mutual belonging. That life-affirming spirit, distinct in each place and common to all places, has endured all the forces of violence intent on its destruction. Those it animates are indeed the *heathens* among us – not the enemies of God but literally 'those who live in the open', outsiders stepping away from the violent script then turning back to face it down.

7. STEALTH

Hope as history.

The Diggers are missing from the typical school history lesson today. If they get a mention at all, it may be just to note that their kind never lasts long; their story is always short and their work forever overwhelmed. Yet here we are sharing their story, and their work was passed on to the generations that followed. Right now, small groups are turning the factory wastelands of Detroit into communal vegetable patches, and abandoned corners of Dundee into free-for-all orchards. Subsistence farmers around the world join as *La Via Campesina*, a global movement of two hundred million land-workers resisting the invasion of corporate agroindustry. The Diggers inspired the Occupy collectives to reclaim for the public the privately-owned squares outside our shopping malls and cathedrals. Now they inspire the climate justice movement as it pitches its tents in the shadows of Babylon's tower and tells the Diggers' story once more. The 'Spirit' that Gerard Winstanley hoped would work again in the hearts of others has run through history like veins through a body. His diminutive republic of hope had been made before his time and will keep being made after our own.

Nonetheless, the typical school history lesson prefers to tell Babylon's own story, so dazzled by the crowns of kings and queens as to pass over the lives on which the royal feet stand. To the scribes of imperial Babylon, as for today's bestseller histories of the Western world, the power that counts is authoritarian: you win when you bend the world to your will, or you lose. History's heathens neither have nor want that kind of bulldozer power. Their work is not to visibly force the world to their hand, but to invisibly enrich the ground underfoot, and for this they trust to faith, stealth, and patience – the power of the powerless.

It is also the power of nature, which does not ask for more. We know that if nature finds a field apparently barren, it will turn it into a forest. It first brings up the buried seeds of the pioneer plants we know as weeds, then comes the scrub, which shelters new saplings, until the whole field burgeons into a canopied home for millions of species. The achievement is as gradual as it is absolute. Nature can only create from what it has, but what it creates enriches what it has. Each step on the way changes the way itself and the whole landscape of what is possible, as newly necessary possibilities open up and spent possibilities are left behind. By stealth and patience – but also work – nature creeps towards its own becoming until, as if suddenly, a breeze is breathing through the impossible forest.

To a casual spectator, the empty field is a hopeless place, which appears as barren today as it will tomorrow. To an attentive witness, perhaps a naturalist like Ashlee Cunsolo or a farmer like Aldo Leopold, the field's emptiness is a wound that already hums with healing life; in the present waits a radically different future. As life fills the field, never slacking yet never hurrying, the spectator dismisses the change as sluggish, not spectacular enough, and boredom drives them away. The witness watches an ever-accelerating race and anticipates, vigilantly and without complacency, the field coming into itself.

In an age of crises, is this enough?

A long succession of small achievements led to an Israeli supreme court order to stop the Shabak's routine torture of Palestinian prisoners. In the beginning the prospect of success seemed barren: the Israeli government just denied the abuse. First, campaigners showed beyond doubt that maltreatment was rife. The Israeli government dismissed it as the work of a few bad apples, so campaigners proved that it was standard practice, and the government insisted that it did not amount to torture. Losing that point too, the government was adamant that torturing insurgents thwarted their networks and protected the Israeli public. Campaigners then filed 150 further petitions on behalf of tortured Palestinians. According to one of the lawyers involved, Jessica Montell, this finally 'wore down the court' until in 1999 it ordered the Shabak to stop. Even now, the Shabak's torture continues, but it is less widely used. The campaign changed the story of what is and is not acceptable, and in practical terms it helped to embarrass and push back the violence of a colonial power. The court victory was only a small step, but a forward one: it counted.

At the beginning, the Shabak's power seemed so absolute that the prospect of successfully challenging it was dismissed as impossible by people who, perhaps, would also struggle to imagine a forest in an empty field. Had the activists waited for the conditions to be just right, they would still be waiting today, but instead they held faith with their 'impossible' work. Each small achievement shifted the ground on which they stood and widened the horizon of what would be possible next. The court ruling to come gradually became thinkable, then possible, then foreseeable, then desirable, and finally an actuality. The worth of each small achievement was only seen later, in the fullness of time, as one shuffling footstep in a long succession of change.

Hope's work takes time; short-cuts are out. The farmer Wendell Berry mentions a hillside, once ruined through overuse, that has taken him seventeen years to restore to health. 'If I had been a millionaire, or if my family had been starving, it would still have taken seventeen years,' he says. The legal campaign to outlaw the worst of the Shabak's torture took about the same time, seventeen years. About seventeen years ago, the people's march against the Iraq War began to turn Western societies against the military adventures of their leaders. Seventeen years ago, the climate emergency was barely a conversation. Only a few scientists and activists even thought about it; they were the loony fringe, ignored by government and laughed at in the press. Now their story of the imperilled earth is an accepted narrative whose bogeyman is swimming into view: an economic system captured by corporate capital and feeding off the lives of the people. 'Nature is never in a hurry,' Wendell observes, and it takes 'proper humility' to work with the land at its own pace, just as hope's work, urgent though it ever is, takes patience.

Even when, as is common, an act of hope falls short of its goal, if it makes something possible that was not possible before then it has already changed the world. It has shifted the ground under everyone, even the powerful, whether or not they happen to notice. The campaign to stop recruiting children for war began in earnest in the 1970s, when it was routine practice for governments to send children to kill and be killed all over the world. Although it was unsafe for young people to buy a pint in a pub, according to British law, it was all right to send them to the 1982 Falklands War. Back then, few people even blinked at the contradiction, and since children are so useful to militaries, campaigners were told they would get nowhere. They set out in hope, nonetheless. First, they convinced the UN to make it a war crime to send anyone aged under 15 into combat; at the time, that was as far as governments were willing to go. It took two more decades to outlaw the use of anyone aged under 18 in war, although the UK and US insisted then, as they have ever since, that they need to recruit at a younger age just to keep their armies going. And yet, after a succession of small changes driven by just a handful of people over four decades, three-quarters of the world's governments now allow recruitment of adults only from age 18. Army generals now concede that it would be wholly wrong to send under-age soldiers into war, a view their predecessors rejected out of hand. More work remains, as always. Today, you can apply to join the British army at age fifteen, sign up on your sixteenth birthday, and learn how to impale a person on a bayonet before you turn 17, ready to do it for real a year later – or have the same done to you. One day, so I hope as one who works on this campaign, no one under the age of 18 will be recruited and trained to kill, and no general will look back with nostalgia on the days they stuffed their ranks with adolescent children to fight their wars for them. But that day is yet to come.

These might be cherrypicked examples of hope's work were it not for similar stories behind all changes for the common good. Our imperfect but real rights to sustenance, to a home, to work with dignity, to learn, to be cared for in health, to have a say in how society works, and to love whom we love, were not handed down to us by kings and queens but gradually wrested from them – and not over 17 years but over 1,700 years and more. That struggle has been peppered with violence, but most of the change has been made through the patience of history by social movements holding faith with their apparently impossible work. Were it not for people of hope confronting the Cold War arms race, we might all have disappeared in a mushroom cloud by now. 'Heathen power', working from the outside in, through the hearts and hands of those like the Diggers who live 'in the open', has not just tweaked society for the better here and there; it has carried us through.

And still all this precious gain is vulnerable. Hope's hidden history has not stopped the institution of violence from inventing new machinery of harm. The bulldozers have not gone away, nor has the capacity to burn the world down from the mental bunkers of Washington, Moscow, and Beijing; meanwhile our societies slip and slide with almost languid ease towards ecological collapse, economic collapse, mass unrest, war. A crux question is whether the same spirit that moved through the Diggers will now quicken our hearts and minds as we face the crises of our times. As to whether that spirit is enough – enough for what? If life deserves love today, is that not enough? Who can say what tomorrow will bring, other than another day when life will still deserve loving? No reassurance here.

Just this. We may harbour hopes that crest and crash to nothing, yet hearing Mansur, still know 'the earth is alive'. When a wound can heal – and not all can – the life around the absence fills it, in faith and stealth, leaving a scar in remembrance of violence and as a testament to renewal. Left to its ways, and even after all the evil pitched against it, the earth would still fill every empty field with a forest, and it has not given up on us just yet. This riven world has always carried possibilities larger than we have known — or can now predict. Life calls out. As Rebecca Solnit has said, if the future is dark like the grave, it is also dark like the womb.

8. TURNING UP

Hope as repentance.

For what has already been lost, hope arrives too late. Africa, the Americas, South Asia were condemned to servitude in the name of civilisation. Dresden, the forests of Vietnam, Fallujah – monstrous violence in the name of peace left them desolate. In the name of progress, the natural world is being drained of its vitality. Everywhere, the poorest are pushed to the edge, reduced to the 'blood price' of prosperity. Violence knows only how to subtract. It punches holes in the fabric of the earth and its people, leaving grievous absences where once life and hope had been; wounds that gape in accusation. Rage, mourn, lament – above all, repent.

And act. After the deluge of violence, the life that remains still makes a claim on us. A parable:

A rich man plunders an old forest until, one morning, only one tree is still alive. That day Optimism and Hope pass each other on the way. Hope: 'You have been here from the beginning, why are you leaving?' Optimism: 'Because only one tree is still alive. What about you – you are so late, why have you come at all?' Hope: 'Because only one tree is still alive.'

Why does Hope bother? Not because the odds of saving the last tree are better than fifty-fifty – that kind of calculation is Optimism's to make. Hope turns up knowing that even one living thing is worthy of love. Unless all is dead, it still has work to do.

So why is Hope so late to arrive? Indeed, where have you and I been while the logging industry has been flattening the world's forests, clearing twenty times the area of Britain in the last thirty years? 'Amazon' is now less likely to call to mind the world's richest ecosystem than its richest retailer, the new global shopping mall. How can hope, yours or mine, face the fact of the dying forest while boxed in by a culture that permits a megacorporation to steal that forest's name without even blinking at the contradiction? No wonder hope arrives late.

Listening to people for whom, as Basma puts it, 'hope is something you make every day', it soon becomes clear that they share something vital in common: they know what they live for. Palestinians know, as does every other people struggling for liberation. Basma's unjustly jailed friend, Mansur, knows, because when he watches the sunrise from his cell, he knows the earth is alive and can live that day through. But our economically advanced societies do not seem to know, not with showboat politician, billionaire media baron, and marketing executive at the helm, who push the lie that the privilege of many choices makes us free and democratic. How can we know either freedom or democracy until we choose, in common, which Amazon is worthy of love and which is not?

Consider George Zabelka, the air force chaplain who, in the name of freedom and democracy, played a small but definite part in the nuclear death of a city. His crushing confession: 'I watched … I knew hundreds of thousands of women and children were vaporised, incinerated, and I said nothing – I was silent.' *I watched, I was silent.* Does this same confession not await the comfortable classes of Western civilisation? George said his military-religious training had left him 'brainwashed'. Only when he stood in the ash did he come back to himself and face the disgrace of his choices. And yet, while he could barely believe he could fall so far short of the life he had meant to live, that life was still within him, as if waiting. Long after leaving the air force, George returned to Japan: 'I fell down on my face and I told [everybody] I wanted to be forgiven for this crime.' Inspired by Martin Luther King, convinced by now that his God is nonviolent, George devoted the rest of his life to peace making; from his tragedy, hope emerged. He came to hope's work late, but he got there.

Our ecological crisis, as possibly the most complex challenge that humanity has ever faced, is now believed by many to be beyond hope's reach. We are all George Zabelka. We – I mean me and perhaps also you – have colluded with such ecological violence that the seas now rise without mercy and the soils get ground to dust. We know that thousands of species are lost every year, forever, and millions of people have already fled the spent land of their homes. We know that air travel, car culture, animal-derived diets, and massive businesses that profit from plunder are still the norm in Babylon. We know that while greenwashing governments levy a charge for plastic bags but still back big oil companies, prop up intensive agriculture, expand airports, and kick off the occasional war of choice, our wayward societies will reap the whirlwind. As the earth burns, so shall the streets, as ecological collapse meets deepening economic segregation and the ever-more forceful disenfranchisement of most of the world's people. And none may object, *We didn't know.*

Babylon's towering socio-economic system continues to corral our mass participation, all in the name of public prosperity but actually for the sake of corporate capital. Statistics show that in the West we spend more time on high street shopping, trash TV, and status updates than anything else outside work, which for millions is reduced to a treadmill to pay the bills or less. This human-made world makes the forest foreign; both words share the same root meaning of 'on the outside'. Few children have ever been introduced to a frog in the wild. They are left instead to kick about after school in an unreal landscape of chain stores, lollipop trees, bolted-down benches, and *No Skateboarding* signs. Will we confront the anti-social behaviour of corporations that urge children to buy belonging for a £100 pair of trainers and exploit other children to sew them together in dollar-a-day sweatshops on the other side of the world? Will we confront the lies that loot children's futures by robbing them of the names of the trees and schooling them instead in the names of every corporate brand? Or are we so 'well-adjusted to injustice', as the philosopher Cornel West has put it, that we will ignore all this to keep calm and carry on?

Thankfully, millions of children and young people hunger to outgrow the corporate-consumer masquerade, fed up with a moribund economic system that tries to cheat them out of knowing what does and does not matter. They, at least, are awake. They, at least, are alive with hope, even as our violence against the earth – yours and mine – fills them with grief. They, at least, have lost neither the spiritual wherewithal to wonder at our teeming soils and seas, nor the sense of justice to know that plunder is a crime. Many people say that wild nature will 'assert itself' by killing off our species, as if this would be a good thing. That might come to pass, but today that same wild nature is beginning to assert itself in the minds and hearts of young people, and still moves in older people who have not lost a feeling for which Amazon is worth loving.

When Greta Thunberg first heard about the prospect of ecological breakdown, at the age of eight, she was flabbergasted to find the adult generation just coasting along with the violence of it:

'I remember thinking it was very strange that humans, who are an animal species among others, could be capable of changing the earth's climate, because if we were ... we wouldn't be talking about anything else. As soon as you turned on the TV everything would be about that ... you'd never read or hear about anything else ...'

In Greta's view, our societies have been too afraid to face this tragedy of our own making. While the tribes of our political class chunter at each other, her generation is doing more than any other to turn us all around. Ranged against them are an armchair army of naysayers who insist that the earth gave us a deadline and we missed it; that all our wind turbines and small sustainable farms are now just chaff in a storm; or that the very idea that human beings can so violate the natural world that it can no longer sustain us is an elaborate hoax. They are mistaken. The choice we face is not climate breakdown yes or no, but how many deadlines we allow ourselves to miss — how far down the slope we are willing to slide in allowing our ecological violence to degrade the great society of the earth. We are coming late indeed to hope's work, but Greta is right — we still need to get to it.

And we can. Our societies have everything we need to move away from habits and unthoughtful beliefs that rest on violence, be it against others or indeed ourselves. We can choose to treasure work that re-enchants us with humanity and earth — through the arts, for example, and rituals that recover the experience of belonging, and perhaps some of the more life-affirming expressions of religious faith. We can choose to forge fellowships that hold hope in common, reaching over the social rifts that injustice has made normal — and to cultivate communities that actually commune, where diversity is not just an abstract idea but a genuine attentiveness to one another. We can choose to build small republics of hope where solidarity with humanity and earth is a conscious practice, and grow social movements prepared to face down the corporate-backed, strongman-showman politics of our age. Especially, we can choose to stand by people boxed in by economics, so that they may be first, and not left to be last, to find the elbow room that life-affirming choices need. And I think we need time, too, to enjoy being the people we are and mean to be, sitting together around the fire, sometimes within the city walls, sometimes in wild places under the sky. Hope is work, but it is also a song.

And it is a journey, through a landscape both traumatised and achingly alive. On one side waits despair, as the belief that nothing can be done, and on the other complacency, as the belief that nothing need be done. Both conspire to ensure that nothing gets done. From time to time, feelings of despair are bound to claim those who mourn the losses, just as the longing to hide from them can be overwhelming too; hope's flight, as Kaethe Weingarten has said, is not always upward. But the unsettling recognition that something waits to be done – by you, by me, by us, and by the healing action of the entire living world – will not go away. Indeed, it will not leave us alone. The strongest testament to our humanity may not be hope's work itself, but the strength of spirit to hold faith with it; to pick up hope again after we have let it fall. Our saving grace is that the will to hope, *sumud*, exists at all. It seems to me that only in the middle space, between despair and complacency, can life even be. All else is drift.

And as hope steps forward, so cynicism retreats, even as it announces the certainty of hope's failure, which it cannot know. Cynicism, which we might define as a wager on losing everything, is always premature while choices still to be made are just that – still to be made. The foregone conclusions that wars are inevitable, the rich will always win, and the time for caring for the earth has passed, are just the noise of a false consciousness. They offer no real refuge from reality. We are, in a sense, condemned to hope.

Yet hope is not, in my own view, an imperative, an *'ought'*, a matter of living correctly, as if it were the logical conclusion of an ethical calculation. Hope is an invitation, a *'could'*, an appeal arising from a feeling for what has worth, a matter of living abundantly. The invitation begins simply enough: with a love for the life in and around us, which is enough to know that its violation needs resisting. Helen Steven put it like this: 'It is this love of the environment we live in, and of the infinite variety of people around me, that inspires in me a deep reverence and gratitude for life, and so moves me to action.' This is the language of vitality embodied – of life on the move, out to enjoy the world and arrest its violation. To be hopeful is to know that grief only comes to those who love. It is to cultivate that love in our own hearts and fellowships. It is to keep alive to the world as a promising place and a tragic place at the same time. It is the readiness to leave false expectations in the past, and to allow the uncertainty of an unknowable future. And it is to move towards acceptance of the cost that all true love exacts. For sure, breaking out of our domesticating social script might well lead to ethically better behaviour: an honest person will try to live humanely and as honest people will try to live socially and ecologically. But I suspect that hope's gifts are richer still – in becoming freer, truer to who we are, and in some way wilder.

Even after all our violence, and after all our societies have done to pave over the promise of this miraculous world, hope keeps olive-deep roots. Hope has been pushing up forever between the gutter and the kerb – in ancient Babylon, in occupied Palestine, even here outside the new shopping mall this evening. Over the heads of the people passing in and out of its portico, a thousand starlings are murmurating. Their nature is to make the most of what they have, however much or little, which is our own true nature also. We have the invitation, we have choices to make, but do we have the heart? We might as well find out. The real sin – the violence – would be not to try. Hope: 'You feel it, you try to catch it, and you try to make it,' says Basma. And then the future can be faced.

EPILOGUE. BURNING HEARTS

The day is late when they finally leave the city behind, though its heat still beats hard at their backs. The air hangs thick with the endless noise, the rush, kicked-up dust, the reek of a rubbish dump.

The man, intent on the puzzle of his thoughts, stops to shake the dust from his feet: 'This place sticks to us even as we leave it.' The woman does the same and they walk on, bowed in dismay, with nowhere to go but away.

Stillness soon falls over them as they wend quietly through woods and fields. The only sound comes from their tread and a few birds still calling long after their season of song. The city's confusion behind them, they are left with their own.

The man is first to speak. 'We were sure. That was our mistake. We had no right to be so sure of ourselves.'

Hope's Work

The woman stops and looks at her friend. 'We were sure of him. I couldn't be sure of more than that. But I believed.'

'And now he's dead,' he replies, bitterly, turning back to face her. In the distance now, the city shimmers on its hill.

'And now we're running away. What right do we have to do that?'

'The right to survive, is what — I don't like it either but we both know they'd have come for us next.'

'So we were wrong?' the woman looks at him. 'You made a promise; we all did.'

The man wonders at the woman. 'You're stronger than I am. I'm glad you are.'

'If I am, I have you and the others to thank for it,' she says, looking back at him, 'and I can't argue with what you're saying.'

She walks on, catching his arm in hers as she goes. The heat has eased, the travellers' shadows grow longer, the vegetation gives out its rank scent.

'I just feel a fool,' continues the man. ' We were called fools often enough.'

' I feel that too, but not as much as guilt,' the woman confesses, looking back the way they had come.' Maybe you're right. We expected too much of that place. And of him. But we could have expected more of ourselves.'

They fall into silence again. The way narrows. Thistles reach over from every crack between stones; soon, but not yet, it will be their time to relax and loose their seeds to the breeze.

' Look,' says the man, who has spotted an abandoned grove of almonds a few yards from their way. He rakes the ground with his fingers in search of last season's nuts, but the woman tells him to look at the tree.' Strange. Why are there so many flowers already? Look up there, those almonds are ready to pick.'

The man stands up to shake the harvest down, and he continues his train of thought.' I just can't get over how easy it was for them to murder him,' he says.' As a soldier I killed people ... the shame of it. But even as he stood before them ... it was like they couldn't see him. How does a man become invisible?'

'Or a woman. It's as he told us. From a tower, however high it is, you see nothing. Only the poor may see clearly.'

'If only! First they came in their multitudes to be with us, and then in their multitudes condemned us – and him. They saw freedom coming and they killed it.'

'They didn't know. Or they were afraid of it. Tell me – when you were a soldier, did you think you could be killed?'

'We all did, every time we went out. The surprise was always coming back alive, then we'd drink like we were trying to finish the job the enemy had left undone.'

'So death is frightening, but so is freedom. It's easier to love the idea of it, talk about it – and then kill it if it comes for you.'

'You sound like him.'

'Because I heard it from him.'

'He always preferred you.'

'I was closer to him, I think, but not close - none of us could get close, not like you and I are now. You know, I think it was your heart he longed for the most.'

The man falls silent, finds a stone and starts cracking the almonds open. The woman sits, takes off her shawl and wraps a blistered foot. He comes over, making a bowl of his smock to carry the nuts, and she takes a fistful.

'Your belief is stronger than mine,' he says, 'I believe and also ... I don't believe.'

She laughs. 'No wonder he liked you. I'm almost the same - I don't believe and yet I do!' She looks at the sun, her dark skin returns its now-softer, now-deeper light. 'Shall we?' And they turn up the path again.

On they go, quietly, the thistly path climbs through a valley marked by a few old trees, squat and twisted by the elements but in full flower. The evening air is still and cool, but the path is still steep enough to bring sweat to the brow.

'We lost, didn't we?' the man begins.

Hope's Work

'Yes,' the woman admits.

'I never felt such longing – drunk on hope, all of us!'

'Yes,' says the woman, with a sad smile, 'that's it exactly. The day's ending, we need to camp.'

'Let's get over that ridge and we'll find water in the next valley.'

'So you have faith in the future after all, my friend,' she smiles, then winces, using his shoulder to take the weight from her feet. 'I'm glad of your shoulder.'

'And I'm glad of yours.'

'So here we are, defeated,' she says, 'grieving his loss, nowhere to go. And yet ...'

'What?'

'Call it folly if you like, but didn't you feel alive?'

'Never more so,' he agrees, and stops himself, suddenly lost in some troubling thought. At length they make the summit ridge of rocks and hardy grasses, and little purple bellflowers with low-hung heads.

She sits on a rock and drinks the last of her water. The

day is nearly done.' Sit for a moment, will you. Look at these little flowers: what are they? How do they survive up here?'

He stoops to take two of them.' Look, meet the soldier in me.' Agitated, he crushes one between finger and thumb.

She watches it fall mutilated into the dust and shakes her head with distaste.' Don't do that,' she says.' Leave the flowers alone. Can't anything be left just to get on with its life? What? What's wrong?'

' War is a cruel teacher, but the best ...'

' Is that what you want me to know? What you saw there?'

' Worse: what I did. War ... it's the worst of us. But more frightening are the pieces of what's left. It's ... when some child I'll never meet doesn't know why he's an orphan.'

' And knowing that the answer to that question ... is you?'

' A stain on your heart. Every time another one,' he finishes.

' But wait ...' she starts, wanting to reassure him, but he stops her gently with a gesture.

' That's what they did to him yesterday,' he says coldly,

intent on the crushed flower at his feet. 'But here's the thing: I keep seeing the executioner. I know who it is under that black hood - it's me - and there's no getting past it.'

He searches her face in defiance. Perhaps he wants her to prove him wrong, but she just holds her hands around his head. 'Let me tell you what I see,' she says. 'When you take off that executioner's hood I see my friend, alive. Beautiful.'

As if their words have exhausted them, more so than the climb and the heat, they sit, side by side, and lean on each other as the sun sinks towards the far hills. The colours of the valley seem strangely bright in the falling light.

'My friend,' she says eventually, 'our cause is lost, we're spent! The future's unthinkable. And still, for all that's happened, there's nowhere I'd rather be in this whole world than right here, now.' She gives him a wry look. 'Let's not kill any more flowers today.'

His smile is sad. 'Let's not.'

He helps his companion to her feet and she waves him

away. 'I'm okay. We never talked about our pasts, did we – we were so in love with what we were doing.' She sets off stiffly. 'Did you know that I was a maid to a prince?'

'No idea!'

'A maid is a nobody. You sit on a feather cushion and live for someone else. I wasn't as beautiful as the others, my skin was too dark for his highness, but he still took me when he wanted his comfort – that's what he called it.'

'I'm sorry, I never asked you.'

She turned to him. 'I was so bitter. It wasn't just that I didn't believe there was anything worth living for – I didn't even want to believe it either. If I hadn't met you and the others, I'd have been in that crowd who condemned him. I'd have cheered his death yesterday and forgotten it today – that's my shame. When I found you all I loved how you talked, the life in your eyes, I wanted to belong so much. But I was afraid – more so then than now. You welcomed me in – all of you – just as I was. I remember you telling me that we were all afraid, it wasn't just me.'

'Yes, I remember.'

'That was when life started for me. So my friend, I can't go back to life as a maid any sooner than you could be a soldier again, living life for someone else.'

'No, we can't go back. And we can't go forward either, now that he's gone.'

'No,' she admits again, 'that's another truth there's no getting past.'

The sun is just setting when a line of trees in the bottom of the valley signals a stream and they take a sheep track down to it. He collects water while she rests her feet and they drink deeply.

Then, a little further down, where the line of trees shades into a wood, they spot a smudge of rising smoke. When they draw near they see a small fire, a pot hung over it, and around it rough mats cut from sacks and three wooden bowls. Keeping their distance, they crouch down to watch. A woman comes out of the trees carrying a bundle of collected logs, which she lets fall at the fire. As she gives the pot a stir, the firelight shows the rips in her clothes, and their once-bright colours now covered in years of grime. In her thick tousled hair she has shoved many found feathers from every kind of bird.

'A witch?' whispers the man to his friend, 'Have you ever seen anyone that old.'

'Maybe a vagabond,' his companion replies. 'Or more – look, three places are set for a meal. Let's be careful.'

The old woman looks through the trees right at them: 'Ba!' she says suddenly, and bids them come out.

'So much for hiding,' says the man, 'let's just say hello and be on our way.'

'Ba,' she says again, bidding them sit and eat. When they join her at the fire the woman tilts the wildness of her head in welcome, and they each press their palms together in thanks, but the two friends have learnt to be wary. The man looks back into the woods for signs of an ambush, but the old woman opens her hands wide to him to say they are alone, and her toothless smile is oddly warm and calming. Then suddenly, eyes wide, hands fixed as talons, she rears up with a hideous noise and roars at the young man like a monster, and as his instinct throws him backwards she apes him, rolling on her back into a hacking laugh, kicking her legs in mirth like a child.

'I think we can relax,' says the younger woman, 'there are no dragons here.' The older looks at the man, but points at the woman and nods her approval.

She dips the bowls into the steaming pot and hands soup to her guests. The travellers can't hide their disappointment when the broth barely fills half a bowl each. The old woman chuckles, rubbing her belly slowly to vouch for her cooking, then chuckles again to some joke of her own. The man fishes in his sack for the almonds, the last of their bread, a few briny olives and a little oil, and they divide it all between them. The old woman softens the bread in her bowl and slurps it down. All three fall into what would be silence, were it not for the slop and slap of the old woman's mouth.

For such little food, the meal leaves them filled. When they finish, it seems they have been eating for a long time, though it can only have been a few minutes. 'Who are ...?' starts the man, but the old woman stops him. She leans forward and opens her mouth wide to show each of them the void where her tongue should be. 'Ba!' she erupts, waving them away as if the injury is an ancient one, but her eyes widen to ask them the same question.

'You don't know what's happened?' asks the younger woman, for the news has been everywhere.

'We're just travellers with nowhere to go,' the man cuts in, wary of giving too much away, but the old woman is still waiting for an answer. 'We've lost a friend,' he offers, 'he was killed.'

'We've nothing left,' adds his companion, 'we're on the run. The rest of us are in hiding.'

'Maybe dead,' says the man. 'Were it not for you we'd go hungry tonight.'

The woman sits back. For a long time, she looks at them by the flickering light of the fire as it spits and crackles. Her smile has gone but something in her eyes holds their hearts aflame.

Later, when they will tell the others, neither will remember how long they sat like this, but it is fully night when the old woman lifts a clean white cloth from a loaf they had not seen. With her talon-fingers she holds the bread above the fire and breaks it in two. As the flames dance, for one passing moment the woman's face is all fire and light. Then she hands the broken loaf to her guests, one half each. 'Ba.'

To show their thanks they lift the bread to eat but she raises a hand to say no, and points between them to bid them back up the hill. She closes her eyes. 'Ba,' she says gently, for it is time to go. The two friends turn to see the narrow path leading back into the darkness, and when they turn back to their host they are astonished, for she has gone.

From the fire they light their lamp and set off through the trees. It is dawn when they reach the city again. The starlings are already flitting from wall to wall and scratching about their feet. Hand in hand, they go in.

NOTES

PROLOGUE: IN THE BEGINNING

The prologue retells and extends a Babylonian creation myth, the *Enuma elish* (c. 1000 BCE). Like other creation myths circulating in the ancient Near East, the *Enuma elish* establishes the order of civilisation through a glorious battle with a dragon. The version here reimagines the heroic story as a tragedy, as if told by Babylon's forgotten dissidents. It makes additional allusions here and there to the Book of Daniel, itself a dissident text composed for a similar imperial context several centuries later.

Babylon means 'heaven's gate'. Its rulers and priests believed the city to be the cosmic centre point, precisely the Altar of Destinies at the heart of the temple sanctum. The 'tower' of Babylon, actually a stepped baked-brick ziggurat rather like a truncated pyramid around 300 feet in height, was said to be the point at which heaven and earth met. To personify the god Marduk on the earthly plane, the king dressed like the god and incorporated the divine name into his own. His semi-divine status was then sanctified in elaborate rites performed by male priests. Babylon's succession of god-king rulers would extend their control through war, or by marrying off their daughters to seal alliances with other kingdoms. Over centuries of near-continuous regional war and upheaval, Babylonia was frequently conquered, too. When the Assyrians took over, they kept the *Enuma elish* as the city's founding story, replacing every mention of Marduk with their own patron deity, Ashur.

Early in the 2003 invasion of Iraq, US forces established a base in Babylon's inner-city complex, whose ruins Saddam Hussein had ordered to be partially reconstructed in his own honour. Today, three corporate oil pipelines run for a mile under the city, between its northern and southern walls; the company's representative, Muayyed al-Sultani, told BBC News that Babylon was now 'just dust' (18 April 2012).

The following excerpts are taken directly from the cuneiform clay tablets on which the *Enuma elish* was recorded, per Nancy Sandars' translation in *Poems of heaven and hell from ancient Mesopotamia* (1971): 'When there was no … no name'; 'Their manners revolt me … have peace'; 'her heart worked'; 'Why must we destroy ... little while'; 'absolute in action'; 'strange and terrible'; 'Give me precedence over ... be law' (re-phrased as 'Make me first of all of you ...'); 'I, not you, will ... to come'; 'split the belly, pierced ... the womb'. 'It shall be Babylon ... the gods'; 'Blood to blood I ... is Man'. 'Green and true' alludes to the *viriditas* or vitality of living things, sometimes translated as 'green truth'.

The passage opening the charismatic Babylonian's defence of the status quo – 'For the great god Marduk ... lord of Babylon' – is a slightly re-phrased translation of a cuneiform inscription found on a cylindrical lapis lazuli seal, meant for the king to wear on a necklace, as cited in Karen Radner, *A Short History of Babylon* (2020). The phrase 'rules only to bless, conquers only to spare' is drawn from the political grandee Thomas Babington Macauley's gushing praise of the British Empire in 1824.

The rest of the Babylonian's speech draws on today's prevailing national security narrative, as articulated by influential voices on the left and right within the political mainstream: 'The weak crumble ... in the end peace is made with the strong.' (Benjamin Netanyahu, Twitter, 29 August 2018); 'End defence austerity and face up rationally to the global chaos.' (Paul Mason, Twitter, 10 October 2017); 'As for the once-mighty British lion, it is now a mangy and malnourished creature. For Britain has run down its defences …' (Melanie Phillips, *Jerusalem Post*, 15 March 2018); 'I believe in American exceptionalism with every fibre of my being.' (Barack Obama, speech at West Point, 28 May 2014); 'We all bleed the same red blood of patriots … Together, we will make America strong again … we will make America great again.' (Donald Trump, first speech as US President, 20 January 2017).

'Great openings' is taken from a line in George Fox's *Journal* (1647): 'And in that I also saw the infinite love of God, and I had great openings.' Eating and working together is borrowed from a vision of Gerrard Winstanley about the faithful community, as discussed in David Boulton, *Gerrard Winstanley and the Republic of Heaven* (2000). One line is taken from the George Miller film, *Mad Max: Beyond Thunderdome*: 'Listen on! Listen on! This is the truth of it.' The same speech continues: 'Fighting leads to killing, and killing gets to warring, and that was damn near the death of us all. Look at us now, busted up and everyone talking about hard rain!'

The characterisation of the dragon as a monster that must be slain for all our sakes follows my own primary school memories of the George and the Dragon story. It is also informed by John Day's discussion of the creature's mythic origins in *God's Conflict with the Dragon and the Sea* (1988), and Seamus Heaney's translation of *Beowulf* (1999), in which a starving slave is blamed for rousing a dragon that the eponymous nobleman then kills. A British Army recruitment poster from the First World War depicts Britain as St George slaying Germany's dragon; another propaganda poster shows a gorilla wearing a German soldier's hat and carrying Britain's women away.

The reference to special forces soldiers storming homes by night is drawn from my conversations with Ben Griffin about his time with the SAS during the Iraq War, also which he also related in a lecture given in Kingston, London, *The Making of a Modern British Soldier* (2015).

CHAPTER 1: LOVE

Harold Wilson referred to the 'white heat' of technological change in a speech about industrial and commercial automation in 1963, where he also said: 'So the choice is … between the blind imposition of technological advance, with all that means in terms of unemployment, and the conscious, planned, purposive use of scientific progress to provide undreamed of living standards and the possibility of leisure ultimately on an unbelievable scale.' The idea that the future has now become 'something to be distracted from' is inspired by Dougald Hine's improvised talk, *Remember the future?* for the Dark Mountain project in 2010.

The Goalkeepers Global Youth Outlook Poll conducted by Ipsos in 2018 found that 42 per cent of adults in the UK said they were optimistic about the future of the world and 29 per cent thought they could make a difference to how the country is governed (versus 56 per cent and 30 per cent, respectively, of children aged 12–15). Common psychological responses to the climate crisis include worry, fear and grief, among others; for example, see Ashlee Cunsolo and Neville Ellis,

'Ecological grief as a mental health response to climate change-related loss', published in *Nature* (2018).

The reference to love as a commitment to one another is inspired by Isabel Carter Heyward, *The Redemption of God: A Theology of Mutual Relation* (1982) and Simone Weil, *Human Personality* (1943), where she wrote: 'The spirit of justice and truth is nothing else but a certain kind of attention, which is pure love.'

The idea that the will to buy one's way to betterment only leads to dissatisfaction is inspired by Wendell Berry, *Two Economies* (2005), published online at the World Wisdom Library: 'The industrial economy … is always striving and failing to make fragments (pieces that it has broken) add up to an ever-fugitive wholeness.'

The quotations of the No Conscription Fellowship are taken from their manifesto, as cited in David Boulton, *Objection Overruled* (1967), and the situation faced by German objectors, many of whom were committed to mental asylums for the apparent 'madness' of their stand, is summarised in a speech by Guido Grünewald, *German resistance to World War One* (2016). In the background to the discussion here is

Mary Glasspool's insight that 'only affirmation can overcome negation', borrowed from her sermon at Christ Church Cathedral in Vancouver for All Souls Day, 2018.

Other sources are as follows. Aldo Leopold is quoted from *The outlook for farm wildlife* (1945). To 'feel the pull of life' is the closing encouragement in Agnes Martin's essay, 'Beauty is the mystery of life' (1989). Thomas Friedman is quoted from *The Lexus and the Olive Tree* (1999). The reference to letting refugees drown alludes to an article by the commentator Katie Hopkins in the *Sun* discussing refugees crossing the Mediterranean: 'Show me bodies floating in water ... I still don't care.' (17 April 2015).

CHAPTER 2: PROMISE

Arundhati Roy is quoted from her speech, *Come September*, which she delivered in Santa Fe in the wake of the 9/11 atrocities in New York and Washington.

CHAPTER 3: FREEDOM

This chapter's 'breakthrough' motif is inspired by Václav Havel's greengrocer parable, and especially Andrew Shanks' discussion of it in *God and Modernity* (1999). Drawing on Jan Patočka's observations on his own experience as a dissident under the Czechoslovakian dictatorship, Shanks proposes that historical crisis may be capable of moving people 'out of the unquestioned prejudices of their culture … into a genuinely open-minded thoughtfulness'. After Patočka, he characterises those who have partly broken out of their prescribed script as 'the shaken'. I have paraphrased Havel's parable and, unlike the original, cast a woman in the greengrocer's role. The Ursus factory anecdote is cited on the Václav Havel website.

'Man is still the first weapon of war' is quoted from the British army booklet, *Soldiering: The Military Covenant* (2000). The notion of a soldier as a weaponised human being is an extension of Roméo Dallaire's use of the term to characterise child soldiers specifically. The military necessity of the 'intense indoctrination' of initial training is argued in McGurk et al., *Military Life: The Psychology of Serving in Peace and Combat* (2006), which cites with approval a list of coercive psychological conditioning techniques used to break down the young mind for military work. The description of basic soldier training is drawn from my research report, *The First Ambush? Effects of Army Training and Employment* (2017). Evidence for the traumatic impact on soldiers of killing and injuring others is summarised in the same report and its companion: *The Last Ambush? Aspects of Mental Health in the British Armed Forces* (2013). Ken Lukowiak's Falklands story is told in his memoir, *A Soldier's Song* (1993); George Zabelka's in the documentary film, *The Reluctant Prophet* (1988); Arthur Galston's is summarised briefly in my book, *Spectacle Reality Resistance: Confronting a Culture of Militarism* (2014), and Ben Griffin's is based on my conversations with him between 2010 and 2019.

The reference to hopeful choices being made alone, but the endeavour being common, is inspired by womanist theologians, for whom 'salvation is always social', according to Monica Coleman in *Making a Way Out of No Way* (2008). It is further inspired by Gillian Rose in *Love's Work* (1995): 'Philosophy intimated the wager of wisdom – as collective endeavour and as solitary predicament.'

The notion that the oppression of the Western middle class is genuine but abstract is borrowed from a 1968 interview with Huey Newton, co-leader of the Black Panther Party, conducted while he was in prison and published in *The Movement*. There he distinguished, but also sought to align, the 'abstract' oppression of white radicals with the 'real' oppression of black radicals: '[We black revolutionaries] are the reality of the oppression. They [white revolutionaries] are not. They are only oppressed in an abstract way; we are oppressed in the real way. We are the real slaves! … Many of the young white revolutionaries realise this and I see no reason not to have a coalition with them.'

The thousands of marketing messages that assail the average Londoner every day are discussed by Owen Gibson in *The Guardian*, 19 November 2005: 'From the Coca-Cola awning at the newsagent's to the looming O2 billboard on the high street, the succession of Calvin Klein ads on the tube escalator and the McDonald's-branded steps, the journey to work becomes a bombardment of marketing messages.'

James Baldwin is quoted from a conversation with Reinhold Niebuhr, cited in James Cone, *The Cross and the Lynching Tree* (2013). 'Knee on the neck' alludes to the killing of George Floyd, who was unarmed, by a white police officer in Minneapolis in 2020; as Floyd lay on the ground, the officer knelt on his neck for several minutes.

Solastalgia is discussed in Glenn Albrecht, 'Solastalgia: The Distress Caused by Environmental Change', *Australasian Psychiatry* (2007).

The discussion of *As You Like It* comes from my own experience of watching the play, particularly Maria Aberg's production for the Royal Shakespeare Company in 2013. I have also drawn on Chris Fitter, *Radical Shakespeare* (2012), and Richard Wilson, '"Like the old Robin Hood": *As You Like It* and the enclosure riots', *Shakespeare Quarterly* (1992). Both writers shed valuable light on the historical context of the play, particularly the enclosures and midland forest society, and offer contrasting views of Shakespeare's sympathy with the rural dispossessed.

CHAPTER 4: DISILLUSION

This chapter's allusions to the behaviour of water are inspired by similar metaphors used by Rosa Luxemburg to describe political change; her quotation is taken from a letter sent from prison to Mathilde Wurm on 16 February 1917. The factual background to the march, including the cited views of activists at the time, draws on Ian Sinclair, *The March That Shook Blair* (2013). That book observes that the only mainstream political leader to join the march – and then reluctantly – was the leader of the Liberal Democrats, who opposed the war on legal grounds alone.

YouGov's *Iraq Tracker* and Ipsos Mori polls found that, in early 2003, three-quarters of the British public were willing to support the invasion of Iraq if it had United Nations approval; and that, after it began without that approval, two-thirds supported it anyway. The polls also found that, more than ten years after the event, most people polled remembered having opposed the war.

Of the 163 countries ranked by the Global Peace Index in 2019, Iraq was ranked 159.

The coining of 'mob' to describe a fickle public is described briefly at Etymonline.com and in Michael Dobson, 'Moving the audience: Shakespeare, the mob, and the promenade', *Shakespeare Bulletin* (2005). The 'futile commotion' of the 'All Fools' Day' march is a remark from a

Spectator article written in 2003 by Lloyd Evans, which goes on: 'What a balm to the suffering suburban heart. How it cheers the soul to take part in this masquerade of revolution. It purges the iniquities imposed every day by "authority". Everyone goes home refreshed, their consciences reborn.'

The notion that the worth of a leader may be measured by their entertainment value, tie choice, or legs, is taken from many British national media stories on the same themes about Boris Johnson, Jeremy Corbyn, Theresa May and Nicola Sturgeon.

The British establishment's anxiety about public opposition to future wars was confirmed in a speech by the Chief of the Defence Staff to the Chatham House thinktank in 2015: *Building a British military fit for future challenges rather than past conflicts.*

Other sources: Martin Luther King is quoted from his autobiography (1998); Primo Levi from *Survival in Auschwitz* (1947); Natalia Ginzburg from her short essay, 'The son of man', in Marjorie Agosin (ed.), *A Map of Hope: Women's Writings on Human Rights* (1999); and Ashlee Cunsolo from 'Climate change as the work of mourning', *Ethics and the Environment*

(2012). The American bombing of date palm groves in Latifiya, Baghdad was reported by Solomon Moore in the *New York Times* (11 January 2008).

CHAPTER 5: FELLOWSHIP

I happened to be sitting nearby when I watched an old man find a frog and show it in silence to his grandchildren, at Ullswater in Cumbria. The notion of 'saturated being' is inspired by a sermon of Martin Luther King, *Unfulfilled Hopes* (1959). The ultra-rational, 'technostrategic' discourse of Cold War nuclear planners is vividly described in Carol Cohn, 'Sex and death in the rational world of defense intellectuals', *Signs* (1987).

The reference to Julian of Norwich alludes to one of her visions or 'showings' (*c.* 1395): 'And in this [God] showed me something small, no bigger than a hazelnut, lying in the palm of my hand, as it seemed to me, and it was as round as a ball ... In this little thing I saw three properties. The first is that God made it, the second is that God loves it, the third is that God preserves it.'

Information about the Shabak has been taken from several sources, including: Eóin Murray and James Mehigan (eds.), *Defending Hope* (2018); Lena Meari, '*Sumud*: A Palestinian philosophy of confrontation in colonial prisons', *South Atlantic Quarterly* (2014); Ilan Pappe, *A History of Modern Palestine* (2nd ed., 2006); and reports of the human rights organisation B'Tselem.

Other sources are as follows. Alice Walker is quoted twice: from an interview with Donna Seaman published online at American Libraries, 8 May 2013, and from the introduction to her book, *Anything We Love Can Be Saved: A Writer's Activism* (1997). The quotes from *Cosmos* are from the opening of the first episode (1980) and the companion book of the same name (1981). Helen Stevens' courtroom statement was made in 1984 and is quoted from *Quaker Faith & Practice*. Joyce Pickard is paraphrased from her contribution to a Quaker meeting in the 2000s. Monica Coleman is quoted from *Making a Way Out of No Way*, op cit. The secret diary in which Julius Fučík detailed his interrogation resistance techniques, *Notes From the Gallows*, has been shared internationally among many dissident movements.

CHAPTER 6: FAITH

The theme of this chapter was decided after a conversation with a friend with Palestinian heritage. When I asked how Palestinians find hope, she replied, 'Well, there's *sumud*.' The writing of Lena Meari and Toine van Teeffelen has also substantially contributed to the appreciation of *sumud* in these pages.

The chapter's opening story is summarised from Eóin Murray, 'Under siege', in *Defending Hope*. Facts related to Israel's invasion of Gaza in 2014 and the Great March of Return in 2018–19 are taken from the UN High Commissioner for Refugees, the UN Human Rights Council commission of inquiry, Human Rights Watch, and K. Elessi et al., 'The effect of the 50-day conflict in Gaza on children: a descriptive study', *Lancet* (2017). Israel's prime minister, Benjamin Netanyahu, is cited in *The Guardian* (10 March 2019). Mirna Bamieh is quoted from a short film, *Saving Palestine's Forgotten Food*, on the *AJ+* site (2019). Other background is based on *A history of modern Palestine*, op cit., and B'Tselem.

The Diggers' quotations are drawn from *Gerrard Winstanley and the Republic of Heaven*, op cit.

CHAPTER 7: STEALTH

The legal campaign to end the Shabak's torture is outlined by Jessica Montell in *Defending Hope*, op. cit.

The brief history of the campaign to stop the use of children for military purposes is based on my experience of working on the campaign, and Jo Becker, 'Campaigning to stop the use of child soldiers', in her *Campaigning for Justice: Human Rights Advocacy in Practice* (2012).

Other sources: Wendell Berry is quoted from a lecture to the Schumacher Society: 'People, land and community' (1981), and Rebecca Solnit from *Hope in the Dark* (2004).

CHAPTER 8: TURNING UP

'Blood price' alludes to a statement in 2001 by the then US Secretary of State, Madeleine Albright, during an interview with the journalist Lesley Stahl. Referring to the impact of economic sanctions on the Iraqi people, Stahl asked: 'We have heard that a half million children have died. I mean, that's more children than died in Hiroshima. And, you know, is the price worth it?' Madeleine Albright answered: 'I think this is a very hard choice, but the price — we think the price is worth it.'

The notion of a felt truth making a claim upon how a person or society lives is drawn from Kimberley Curtis' critical appreciation of Hannah Arendt, *Our Sense of the Real* (1999), while the reference to modernity's urban centres as 'unreal' is taken from the long essay by the Scottish poet Iain Crichton Smith, *Real people in a real place* (1986).

In Jürgen Moltmann's *Theology of Hope* (1967) I found an echo of the idea that cynicism and complacency are 'premature': 'Presumption is a premature, selfwilled anticipation of the fulfilment of what we hope for from God. Despair is the premature, arbitrary anticipation of the non-fulfilment of what we hope for from God.'

My characterisation of freedom as authenticity and of hope's work as an expression of freedom is inspired by many people, including Václav Havel in *The Power of the Powerless*, already mentioned; also Ben Okri, *A Way of Being Free* (1997); Paulo Freire's characterisation of emancipatory education as a 'humanising vocation' that tends towards the recovery of our 'stolen humanity' in *Pedagogy of the Oppressed* (1970); Ursula Le

Guin's ingenious critique of consumer capitalism in *The Dispossessed* (1974); Alice Walker's poem, 'Hope is a woman who has lost her fear' (2013); and the opening words of Ernst Bloch's *The principle of hope* (1954): 'I move. From early on we are searching. All we do is crave, cry out. Do not have what we want.'

Other sources: George Zabelka is quoted from the documentary film, *The Reluctant Prophet* (1988); the devastation of the world's forests – 4.2 million square kilometres lost since 1990 – is attested in a report of the United Nations Food and Agriculture Organisation, *State of the world's forests* (2020); Greta Thunberg's words are taken from her vivid TEDx talk in Stockholm a few months into her school strike in 2018; Helen Steven is quoted from her obituary by Kathy Galloway, online at the Dangerous Women Project (2016); Kaethe Weingarten is quoted from a paper presented in Reykjavik in 2006, *Hope in a Time of Global Despair*; and Cornel West is quoted from *Hope on a Tightrope* (2008).

EPILOGUE: BURNING HEARTS

The epilogue reimagines the biblical story of two disciples who flee Jerusalem after Jesus' death, their hopes in ruins (Luke 24:13–35). They are greeted on the way by a stranger, who reveals to them that Jesus' death is part of hope's story in the world. Later, the two disciples recall: 'Did not our heart burn within us, while he talked with us on the way …?' Come evening, the company sit to eat and when the stranger breaks bread they realise he is Jesus, who then vanishes. Now aware that the source of their hope abides with them always – and that this has been the meaning of the gospel all along – the companions return to the city to begin again.

Much Christian commentary and art has assumed that the two disciples are men, but the biblical story only gives one a name; the other could be a woman, and both could be of any age and background. This retelling, like the biblical story, takes place just after Jesus' crucifixion in spring, but otherwise the place and time are left to the reader's imagination. Jesus' disguise as the old woman is inspired in part by Jacquelyn Grant's claim that the nature of Christ is closest to that of a black woman, as cited in Monica Coleman, *Making a Way Out of No Way*, op cit., although here the woman's background is left for the reader to imagine. Perhaps she is not Jesus in disguise after all, but just the person she appears to be.

The reference to almonds budding, flowering and fruiting at the same time is drawn from the Book of Numbers, chapters 17–18, in which this miracle communicates to Aaron that his tribe shall serve as priests at the altar.

THANKS

Like any book, this one is the outcome of so many rich encounters over time that I could not call myself its only author, nor would I want to. It belongs as much to those who have been willing to tell me their stories and allow me to write about them, particularly Basma Bodabos and Ben Griffin, whose personal journeys schooled me early on in hope in the face of violence. I am especially grateful also to Emily Johns, whose engraving on the book's cover speaks for hope at least as well as anything I have written inside it. Elizabeth Baxter at Holy Rood House in Thirsk enthusiastically encouraged me in the work at an early stage and kindly offered me the opportunity to share some initial ideas with the community there. Several early readers supported me, through their belief and sometimes their doubt, to move the book on from a much rougher draft, namely Feryal Awan, Jonathan Baxter, Basma Bodabos, Emily Bowden, Simon Fisher, Caitlin Knights, Rhianna Louise, Irina Luca,

Edouard Mathieu, Tanya Meditzky, Virginia Moffatt, Harriet Proudfoot, Haifa Rashed, Lydia Ratto, Bea Shelley, Rachel Taylor, Sunniva Taylor, Ersilia Verlinghieri, Sarah Voss, Max Whitby, and my writing group, the Musky Writers. Louisa Wright's thoughtful editorial advice was especially valuable, again.

I am grateful to David Moloney and all at Darton, Longman and Todd for being willing to usher this book into being, and for their encouragement and thoughtfulness throughout. And to Peggy Seeger for allowing us to quote a quatrain from her song about the earth, *The Mother*.

While I struggled for a while financially to continue with the work, a number of friends and a few strangers made generous donations to keep me going: Ahlyah Ali, Gail Anderson, Claire Barber, Jonathan Baxter, Jonna Bjornsterna, Ivan Campbell, Bob Cummins, Hubert Cassel, Kevin O'Dell, Sara Gibbs, Dave Green, Birgit Felleisen, Simon Fisher, Laura Griffiths, Jo Hamilton, Rachael Harrison, Iain Lang, Rhianna Louise, Irina Luca, Kate Maclean, Celia McKeon, Tanya Meditzky, Lianne Minasian, Ed Mathieu, Kate Milward, Andrew Morrey, Harriet Proudfoot, Haifa Rashed, Wendy Rashed, Stefan Săftescu, Emma Sangster, Rachel Taylor,

Thanks

Sunniva Taylor, Sarah Voss, Vron Ware, Max Whitby, Joanna Wright, Jo Young, a few anonymous donors who know who they are, and Ron Gooding, who spent a day keeping my boat shipshape and let me off the bill.

I give thanks for all the life – those named here, others unnamed, the turning earth, and perhaps the Spirit of which Gerrard Winstanley once wrote – that has touched me in the making of this book.